THE FORMATION OF
THE GOSPEL TRADITION

THE FORMATION OF THE
GOSPEL TRADITION

EIGHT LECTURES

VINCENT TAYLOR

Ph.D., (London), Hon. D.D. (Leeds), Hon. D.D. (Dublin),
Hon. D.D. (Glasgow) F.B.A.

FORMERLY PRINCIPAL AND FERENS PROFESSOR
OF NEW TESTAMENT LANGUAGE AND LITERATURE, WESLEY COLLEGE,
HEADINGLEY, LEEDS.

MACMILLAN
London · Melbourne · Toronto

ST MARTIN'S PRESS
New York
1968

First Edition, 1933
Second Edition, 1935
Reprinted 1945, 1949, 1953, 1957, 1960, 1964, 1968

Published by
MACMILLAN & CO LTD
Little Essex Street London WC2
and also at Bombay Calcutta and Madras
Macmillan South Africa (Publishers) Pty Ltd Johannesburg
The Macmillan Company of Australia Pty Ltd Melbourne
The Macmillan Company of Canada Ltd Toronto
St Martin's Press Inc New York

Printed in Great Britain by
ROBERT MACLEHOSE AND CO LTD
The University Press, Glasgow

PREFACE

THE following Lectures were given in the University of Leeds during the Spring Term of 1932 at the invitation of the Vice-Chancellor and the Public Lectures Committee, and they are printed as they were delivered apart from sections which had to be omitted and a few subsequent additions.

The subject of the formation of the Gospel tradition is one that has attracted a good deal of attention on the Continent in recent years, and several important discussions have appeared which have not been translated into English. I have devoted special attention to Professor Rudolf Bultmann's *Die Geschichte der synoptischen Tradition* which has recently appeared in its second edition. However his conclusions are estimated it is impossible to doubt the importance of his work and the influence it will exert on the study of the Gospels. This influence is visible, for example, in Professor J. M. Creed's recent valuable commentary, *The Gospel according to St. Luke.* Form-Criticism has attracted too little attention in Great Britain, and I hope that these Lectures will do something to fill a gap in our discussions. While adopting a critical attitude towards the new method, which in truth has severe limitations, I have been glad to develop several suggestions which are prompted by it, and which seem to me to illuminate the larger subject of Gospel

Origins. Lectures provide a useful medium by means of which to put forward suggestions of this kind, especially when they call for further study and consideration by others. If in the hands of Professor Bultmann Form-Criticism has taken a sceptical direction, this is not the necessary trend of the method; on the contrary, when its limitations are recognised, Form-Criticism seems to me to furnish constructive suggestions which in many ways confirm the historical trustworthiness of the Gospel tradition. The special attractiveness of the new method is that, for all its formal and academic character, it forces us to read the Gospels in the closest connexion with the life and experience of the first Christians, and brings the Gospels and the Epistles into nearer relationships. It is the paradox of Form-Criticism that a study which has so much to do with forms should raise such vital issues.

I welcome the opportunity of acknowledging my debt to the scholars whose names I have mentioned above. I regret that Dr. T. W. Manson's important work, *The Teaching of Jesus*, did not come into my hands until the present Lectures had been written ; but, on this account, I am glad to have his strong and independent support on several points connected with the sayings of Jesus.

To the Rev. S. G. Dimond, M.A., and to my wife, I am indebted for help in the reading of the proof-sheets.

VINCENT TAYLOR

Wesley College,
Headingley, Leeds.

PREFACE TO THE SECOND EDITION

I AM glad to avail myself of the opportunity which the second edition of this work affords to refer to some of the literature on Form-Criticism and allied themes which has been published since the book first appeared. Outstanding interest belongs to Professor B. Lee Woolf's translation, under the title *From Tradition to Gospel*, of the second edition of Dibelius's *Die Formgeschichte des Evangeliums* (1933). Professor F. C. Grant, Dean of Seabury-Western Theological Seminary, Evanston, has also placed us deeply in his debt by his *Growth of the Gospels* (1933), and by his *Form Criticism* (1934) in which he supplies a translation of Bultmann's *Die Erforschung der synoptischen Evangelien* (2nd ed. 1930) and Kundsin's *Das Urchristentum im Lichte der Evangelienforschung* (1928). In *Jesus and the Word* (1935) Bultmann's *Jesus* has also been ably translated by L. P. Smith and E. Huntress of Wellesley College, Wellesley, Massachusetts. From Finland comes Johannes Sundwall's *Die Zusammensetzung des Markusevangeliums* (1934) which rests upon the work of Bultmann and other Form-critics and gives special attention to the structure of Mark. H. K. Luce's valuable commentary on Luke (1933) in the *Cambridge Greek Testament* Series also reflects the interest of the new approach to the Synoptic Problem.

Reference must further be made to the series of articles in the *Expository Times* (vol. xlvi, 1934-5) under the title *Some Outstanding New Testament Problems*, and in particular to those of J. M. Creed, *'L' and the Structure of the Lucan Gospel: A Study of the Proto-Luke Hypothesis* (pp. 101-7), A. M. Perry, *Luke's Disputed Passion-Source* (pp. 256-60), and F. C. Grant, *Further Thoughts on the M-Hypothesis* (pp. 438-45).

The present edition is in the main a reprint of the original work. I have introduced a few corrections and alterations, and have supplied an Index of Names and Subjects. The most important alteration is on p. 49f. where, in connexion with Bussmann's discussion of I Cor. xv. 3 f., I have transferred what was formerly footnote 2 on p. 49 into the text. In view of criticisms which have been made with regard to Appendix B, I should like to emphasize the fact that the aim of the experiment described is not to attempt to reproduce the conditions of the Gospel period, but simply to ascertain what are the tendencies of oral transmission. Independent experiments will, I am sure, show that, in spite of additions, the tendencies are definitely towards *abbreviation* and the attainment of a rounded form from which place-names, names of persons, and examples of direct speech tend to disappear, except when an original story is reproduced with a conscious artistic purpose. The only other point to which I wish to refer is the question of the Markan order. It is a mistaken procedure to infer from the adoption of Form-critical principles, or from the mere application of Wrede's theory of the Messianic Secret, that Mark's outline is a purely artificial structure.   On this subject some of the last words from the pen of the late F. C. Burkitt have great force.   In reviewing Sundwall's *Die Zusammensetzung des Markus-evangeliums* in the *Journal of Theological Studies* (April, 1935, pp. 186-8) Burkitt wrote: 'In opposition to the opinion of many scholars I feel that Mark *is* a Biography, if by Biography we mean the chief outlines of a career, rather than a static characterization.   In Mark there is movement and progression. . . .   It does not sound to me like *Gemeindetheologie*, the unconscious secretion of a community of believers.   Nothing but a strong element of personal reminiscence could have produced it.   And therefore I still hold to the belief that it embodies the private reminiscences of Peter, supplemented for the last week by the reminiscences of the young Mark himself.'   In no way, it seems to me, does Form-Criticism weaken this judgment.

VINCENT TAYLOR

Wesley College,
Headingley, Leeds,
July 1935.

CONTENTS

LIST OF ABBREVIATIONS

Albertz, M.	*Die synoptischen Streitgespräche*, 1921.	*S.S.*
Bertram, G.	*Die Leidensgeschichte Jesu und der Christuskult*, 1922.	*L.J.C.*
Bultmann, R.	*Die Geschichte der synoptischen Tradition*, 1921, 2nd ed. 1931.	*G.S.T.*
	Jesus, 1925.	*J.*
	Die Erforschung der synoptischen Evangelien, 2nd ed. 1930.	*E.S.E.*
Burney, C. F.	*The Poetry of our Lord*, 1925.	*P.L.*
Bussmann, W.	*Synoptische Studien*, i.-iii. 1925-31.	*S.Sn.*
Dibelius, M.	*Die Formgeschichte des Evangeliums*, 1919.	*F.E.*
Easton, B. S.	*The Gospel before the Gospels*, 1928.	*G.G.*
	Christ in the Gospels, 1930.	*C.G.*
Fascher, E.	*Die formgeschichtliche Methode*, 1924.	*F.M.*
Fiebig, P.	*Die Erzählungsstil der Evangelien*, 1925.	*E.E.*
James, M. R.	*The Apocryphal New Testament*, 1924.	*A.N.T.*
Koehler, L.	*Das formgeschichtliche Problem des N.T.*, 1927.	*F.P.*
Manson, T. W.	*The Teaching of Jesus*, 1931.	*T.J.*
Meyer, A.	*Die Entstehung des Markusevangeliums*, 1927.	*E.M.*
Meyer, Ed.	*Ursprung und Anfänge des Christentums*, i.-iii. 1921-3.	*U.A.*
Sanday, W. (ed.)	*Oxford Studies in the Synoptic Problem*, 1911.	*O.S.*
Schmidt, K. L.	*Der Rahmen der Geschichte Jesu*, 1919.	*R.G.J.*
Streeter, B. H.	*The Four Gospels*, 1924.	*F.G.*
Taylor, V.	*Behind the Third Gospel*, 1926.	*B.T.G.*
	The Gospels, 1930	*G.*
Windisch, H.	*Der Johanneische Erzählungsstil*, 1923.	*J.E.*

Expository Times.	*E.T.*	*Journal of Theological Studies.*	*J.T.S.*
Hibbert Journal.	*H.J.*	*Theologische Rundschau.*	*T.R.*

I

A SURVEY OF RECENT RESEARCH

In treating the subject of these lectures I desire at the outset to define the nature of the inquiry. By the 'Gospel tradition' I mean that which we have received from the first Christians concerning the words and deeds of Jesus; and by its 'formation' I understand both the external characteristics of the tradition and the process by which it came into being.

It is important that we should appreciate the distinction between the 'Gospel tradition' and the Gospels. Before the Gospels were written the 'tradition' was organic; it was a thing of life, and as such was always changing and growing. Just because of this it was subject to the accidents and experiences of life; it could be corrupted, but it was also capable, through growth and change, of becoming more truly itself, as the sapling grows into the tree and as the child becomes the man. In the Gospels the 'tradition' has attained a relatively fixed formation; it is no longer subject to change, except as it is altered by copyists or by the writers of the later Apocryphal Gospels. Whenever we return to our Gospels we find the tradition as we left it, and the only changes which can happen are those which take place within our own minds through fuller knowledge and understanding. Before these books were written the

A

position must have been very different.   At that time
the tradition was more plastic; it was a story of life and
a product of life; its formation was determined by its
contents and by the mental and spiritual environment
in which it lived; it grew, and developed, and had a
history.

It is this history which I shall attempt to describe in
its various stages in the present lectures.   How far this
is possible remains to be seen; but we can be sure that
there is a story to be traced, and that it can be told, so far
as our methods are adequate and our knowledge and insight permit.

Such a study is foreclosed for those who hold a rigid
theory of Inspiration.   For them the record comes
direct from God; the Gospel is to be received and interpreted, but not to be analysed or traced.   For most of us
this is an impossible conception because it does not take
account of facts.   We gladly recognize the divine element in the Gospels, but we see that they came into existence in human ways, that in His wisdom God did not
think it necessary to safeguard them by protective meas-
ures, but left them free to win their own way and to
make their own conquests.   We believe also that, while
the results of this method are often perplexing to us,
God's way has proved to be to His greater praise and
glory.   But if this is so it is all the more necessary to
understand the process by which the tradition has been
formed and transmitted.

Before the nineteenth century the investigation of the
formation of the Gospel tradition was almost impossible;
ignorance and false views of Inspiration barred the way;

and it is only in comparatively modern times that the attempt has been seriously made. The new science is still young, and in consequence many steps must be tentative. We of to-day are responsible only for the progress it is ours to make, and when we have finished our task we must give place to others. In this sense the inquiry is scientific, although it cannot have the precision possible when things are measured, weighed, and treated in test-tubes.

I

In any inquiry it is essential to know what has already been attempted and achieved. The successful pioneers spare us the necessity of repeating finished tasks, and point the way to new fields. But it is almost as valuable to know the failures of the past, since in this, as in most areas of research, we succeed by our failures. Scholars who have failed to establish a hypothesis are our benefactors; they stand at the end of lanes we might otherwise be tempted to explore and tell us that these are bypaths. Because of this, I propose in this opening lecture to give some account of past research, and especially of its less known and more recent phases. These researches concern the study of the text of the Gospels, the sources on which they rest, the principles of Literary and Historical Criticism, and the investigation of the form or structure of the tradition as it is pursued by the modern *formgeschichtliche* School.

Since the story of Textual Criticism has been so often told, I need not do more than remind you of its importance for our inquiry. So long as ancient records were copied by hand the risks of textual corruption were great; it is very difficult to copy a long document correctly, and corrupt copies become further corrupted in the process of transmission.   In consequence, for the Gospels as for all ancient writings, investigations which seek to recover as far as possible the original text are as necessary as they are difficult.   The abundance of ancient manuscripts, far greater in the case of the Gospels than in any other ancient writings, makes the task at once more arduous and more hopeful, since among thousands of manuscripts it is not likely that the true reading is irretrievably lost.   It is pleasing to remember that in these researches British scholars have taken a leading part.   So successful have the investigations proved that, apart from matters of detail, we can assume the substantial accuracy of the Westcott and Hort text which needs modification in certain directions only, and that mainly as the result of evidence supplied by manuscripts discovered since 1881.   For our special purpose, however, readings which are not original are often of much importance; because they show how the Gospels were understood by copyists in later times, and because existing oral tradition is sometimes revealed by the additions, as, for example, when Codex Bezae adds after Lk. vi. 4 the story of the Man working on the Sabbath.   Textual Criticism is also of great interest because in its most recent phases the tendency is to emphasize the part played by the Great Churches of Early Christianity in the formation of the text.   It is a pleasing sign of the unity of critical research that the influence of different primitive communities is also revealed by Source Criticism, and,

as we shall see, by the study of the earliest Passion-narratives.

I can spare only a few words for the story of Source
Criticism, fascinating and important as it is.   For details I must refer you to the classical works of J. C. Hawkins, J. Moffatt, V. H. Stanton, and B. H. Streeter.   A
century of sustained effort has left certain results firmly
entrenched, although attempts to develop them are still
in progress.   It is almost universally accepted that the
Gospel of Mark, in substantially its present form, was
used by the later Evangelists, Matthew, Luke, and
John.   It is also very widely believed that Matthew and
Luke used a second source, consisting mainly of the sayings of Jesus, and usually known as Q (*Quelle*). This is
the famous Two-Document Hypothesis which is the
foundation of Synoptic research.   Besides Mark and Q
other sources have been suggested in order to explain
difficulties left over by the foundation hypothesis and in
order to account for the material peculiar to Matthew
and Luke.   Thus, both B. H. Streeter and W. Bussmann have found reason to presuppose a source M,
consisting of sayings and parables, which was used by
Matthew, and very many scholars have argued that
Luke used a source L which contained sayings, parables,
and narratives.   In 1924 Streeter put forward a Four-
Document Hypothesis, and Bussmann has more recently (1931) propounded an Eight-Source Theory.   It
is misleading to say that the further hypotheses 'go beyond the clear evidence of the existing documents'.[1]   Of

[1]Cf. Sir Edwyn Hoskyns and Noel Davey, *The Riddle of the New
Testament*, 1931, p. 104.

course they go beyond the existing evidence, but they also arise out of it, and go beyond it only in the sense that any hypothesis transcends the facts it seeks to explain.   Some form both of the M and the L Hypotheses will, I believe, be a permanent gain to Synoptic Criticism, but it remains a matter for further inquiry whether M is a unity, and whether L is more than a cycle of oral tradition.

Besides isolating sources, scholars have sought to discover the manner in which the sources were used; and this, too, is a matter which bears closely on the study of the formation of the Gospel tradition.   So far as Matthew is concerned, agreement is almost unanimous. Matthew used the Gospel of Mark as his fundamental source, re-arranging its order to some extent and inserting into the framework thus supplied material from Q, M, and oral tradition.   Until about a decade ago it was thought that Luke had followed a similar plan, with the qualification that his method was to insert material from Q and his special source mainly at two places in the Markan outline, after the Call of the Twelve (Mk. iii. 13-9) and at the beginning of the account of the last journey to Jerusalem (Mk. x. 1ff).   But in 1921 Canon Streeter startled us by the suggestion that we should reverse this hypothesis.   Q and L, he claimed, were first combined to form Proto-Luke, independent of and slightly earlier than Mark, and it was at a later time that Luke supplemented Proto-Luke by extracts from Mark and the Birth Stories of Lk. i. and ii., and in this way constructed our present Third Gospel.   Elsewhere, in *Behind the Third Gospel*, 1926, I have subjected this interesting and important suggestion to a detailed investigation, and I am convinced that it is sound. The hypothesis has been accepted by many scholars but is rejected by others mainly of the Cambridge School. J. M. Creed, for example, in his important commentary on Luke, 1930, registers his dissent, but the reasons given are inadequate.[1] If the Proto-Luke Hypothesis is accepted, valuable results follow for the study of Gospel Origins; for in this case, in Proto-Luke and Mark, we have two documents containing a sketch of the Story of Jesus, each earlier than 70 A.D. and reflecting different cycles of tradition. The same claim can be made for the four sources, Q, Mark, L, and M. If the tradition itself is likened to a living tree, the sources represent its main branches, or—to put it better—cross-sections of those branches. We can study them and see what differences they contain, and how far they support similar inferences regarding the life of the whole. Used in this way Source Criticism must always be one of the most effective methods of studying the formation of the Gospel tradition; and it is important to urge this in view of the neglect of this method by recent exponents of Form Criticism.

Besides Literary Criticism of the kind just indicated Historical Criticism has long been applied to the study of the documents. Indeed, it is not always realized how much Historical Criticism in general owes to principles which were first hammered out on the anvil of Biblical Criticism. The material contained in the Gospels has been read in the light of contemporary move-

[1]See Appendix A.   See also *E.T.*, xlvi, pp. 101-7, 236-8, 378f.

ments outside Christianity and has been subjected to the tests by which all historical writings must be judged. In recent years especially this inquiry has been pursued with unflagging zeal by R. Reitzenstein, W. Bousset, A. Olrik, O. Weinreich, M. Lidzbarski, P. Fiebig, and others.   Narratives bearing any resemblance to those in the Gospels have been examined in the literatures of Greece, Egypt, India, and China.   In like manner sayings analogous to those of Jesus have been investigated in the Rabbinical literature, the Hermetic writings, and the sacred books of Mandaism.   Even the traditions of later times, such as those which have gathered round the name of Francis of Assisi, have been scrutinized in the hope that they may furnish a basis of comparison.   Folk-tales, Faust stories, and legends of the saints have been examined in order to discover 'laws' of popular poetry and tradition, and miracle-stories and the records of modern psychotherapy have been assembled as a background against which the healing ministry of Jesus may be viewed.   While researches of this kind have sometimes led to wild and ephemeral hypotheses, they have also furnished suggestions which help us more intelligently to understand the formation of the Gospel tradition: we no longer study the Gospels in isolation, but in relation to a body of analogous material which increases in volume every year.   Nor can it be said that the Gospels suffer from comparisons of the kind; on the contrary, the reverse is true.   If there are losses, there are also gains, and the gains exceed the losses.   If one thing emerges from Historical Criticism more than another it is the distinctiveness and originality of the

Gospels.   We compare these books with everything else on earth, only to find that there is nothing quite like them.

II

I will now describe certain investigations which have been in progress in Germany during the last sixteen years, and which are coming to be known as Form-Criticism.   If I devote what may seem a disproportionate amount of attention to this movement, it is not because I hold an exaggerated estimate of its importance, or think of it as supplying a master-key which is likely to end all our difficulties.   In these lectures I shall often have occasion to refer to Form-Criticism in terms of appreciation, because I believe that in many ways it affords real help in the task of tracing the formation of the Gospel tradition; but I shall also indicate the criticisms to which it is exposed.   The reason why I now present a detailed account of the work of this school is because its labours are too little known.   Many of the books in which it may be studied have not been translated into English, and, apart from these, we are dependent on articles[1] in the learned press and on a valuable book by the American scholar, B. S. Easton, *The Gospel before the Gospels* (1928).

The nature of the new study is partly revealed by its forbidding name: *formgeschichtliche*.   This adjective recalls others such as *literaturgeschichtliche* and *religionsgeschichtliche*, to which we have at least become reconciled.   These earlier immigrants denote methods of

---

[1]Cf. *Theology*, May, 1925.   Dr. W. K. L. Clarke's article is now reprinted in his *New Testament Problems*, 1929, pp. 18-24.   See the reference to further books and articles in the Second Preface.

study which proceed, in the one case, from the stand-point of literary criticism and, in the other case, from that of comparative religion.   In the same way *form-geschichtliche* suggests a method which concentrates on the form or structure of the primitive Gospel tradition. For such an investigation Form-Criticism is perhaps the best British equivalent.

Let me explain at the outset that Form-Criticism is primarily concerned with the oral period, although, in the nature of things, it is compelled to take its point of departure from the Synoptic Gospels.   The basal as-sumption is that during this period the tradition circu-lated mainly in separate oral units which can be classified according to their form.   It is believed, further, that much may be inferred regarding the origin of these units, the causes which gave rise to them, and the changes they underwent until in course of time they were given a written form.

I have elsewhere described the new study as 'the child of disappointment' (*G*. 16).   This, I think, is a true characterisation.   The results gained from the Two-Document Hypothesis were good, but gaps still remained in the history of Gospel Origins.   Planks like the *Ur-Markus* Theory and the idea of a lost Hebrew Gospel were thrust forward, only to collapse under the feet of later travellers, so that research seemed called to a halt unless new methods could be devised.   Form-Criticism is an attempt to supply such a method.   This, however, is not the only cause of its emergence.   The method had already been applied by H. Gunkel to the elucidation of the narratives of Genesis, and by other investigators in the field of Greek literature.   Gunkel had inquired concerning the *Sitz im Leben*, the life-situation, out of which ancient tales had sprung, and it was only a matter of time before similar inquiries should be made by himself and others with respect to the New Testament material.   It is with justice, therefore, that L. Koehler speaks of Form-Criticism as the child of Gunkel's spirit (*F.P.* 7).   Other investigators also had prepared the way.   Wrede laid remorseless hands on the Gospel of Mark, beloved of the Liberal-Jesus-Research-School, and sought to trace the influence of dogmatic ideas in its construction.   Schweitzer also pointed out gaps in the Markan outline: 'every section', he said, 'is a station, and the connexions are not guaranteed'.   Wellhausen emphasized the influence of the theology of the primitive community on the existing form of the narratives and sayings of Jesus, and J. Weiss endeavoured to recover the 'oldest Gospel' by a process of sifting and elimination.   It was inevitable that the problem of Gospel Origins, attacked thus from different sides, should become the object of a more complete assault, and it can be no matter for surprise that the *formgeschichtliche* school sprang suddenly into existence, without collaboration from its leaders, who simultaneously pitched their tents before what had seemed the forbidden city.

The pioneer of the new school is M. Dibelius of Heidelberg, who in 1919 published a brief but highly suggestive work under the title *Die Formgeschichte des Evangeliums*.   There can be little doubt that when the historian of contemporary criticism makes up his account high praise will be awarded to this slim volume of about a hundred pages. Dibelius is a pathfinder. Like a traveller who tells of buried treasure he summons us to a fascinating investigation, and gives us reason to believe that, after inevitable disappointments, the expedition will prove well worth while. The Synoptic material is treated only in part, but clear indications are given of formal distinctions between different types of narrative. Dibelius uses both an analytical and a constructive method. He not only discusses the literary phenomena, but also traces the different forms to definite types of people in the Early Church, to preachers, narrators, missionaries, and teachers. He affirms the importance of the Christian Mission itself in the formation of the tradition, and especially emphasizes the influence of preaching. 'In the beginning was the sermon' is, as E. Fascher says, the foundation thesis (*F.M.* 54). The Evangelists, Dibelius maintains, were only in the smallest degree authors, they were rather collectors of units of tradition existing in free circulation. It was in the process of circulation that the units were formed. Just as during the War recruiting-speeches and appeals for War Loan gained definite formal characteristics, so in the first preaching traditional stories took form and shape. We have to admit the paradox that 'unliterary men created a style' (*F.E.* 15).

While Dibelius was writing his book there was already in existence, though still unpublished, a manuscript which was to prove of great value to the new study. This was a critical examination of the Synoptic framework published by K. L. Schmidt in 1919 under the title *Der Rahmen der Geschichte Jesu*. In the opinion of some, Schmidt's investigation has completely shattered the Synoptic framework and shown that it is a purely artificial construction.   Time, I am sure, will qualify this opinion, but there can be no doubt that Schmidt has provided strong support for the basal assumption of *Formgeschichte*, that originally the Gospel tradition consisted of fragments in free circulation. Towards the material itself Schmidt's attitude is conservative, but his rejection of the outline is radical.   'The stories of Jesus', he writes, 'lie for the most part on one and the same plane.   Only now and then, from considerations about the inner character of a story, can we fix these somewhat more precisely in respect of time and place.   But as a whole there is no Life of Jesus in the sense of an evolving biography, no chronological sketch of the Story of Jesus, but only single stories, *pericopae*, which are put into a framework' (*R.G.J.* 317).   The exception to this state of affairs is the Passion-narrative, which Schmidt thinks attained a continuous form at an early period, and in this opinion Dibelius, and to some extent Bultmann, concur.

During the same period R. Bultmann, now of Marburg, had independently been attacking the problems of form, and in 1921 he published his book *Die Geschichte der synoptischen Tradition*.   This work, one of the most important contributions to Gospel Criticism which have appeared in our time, is in many respects very different from that of Dibelius.   It is more detailed and its aim is fuller: in about 230 pages it attempts to trace the origin and formation of the material from the oral period to the written Gospels.   Further, its tone and tendencies

are different. Dibelius is liberal rather than radical;
Bultmann is radical to the point of scepticism, and it is
not strange that he has been looked upon as *Strauss
Redivivus*. If Bultmann is right, we have not only lost
the Synoptic framework but also much the greater part
of the material. The narratives are mainly legends and
ideal constructions, and most of the sayings, while Palestinian in origin, are products of primitive Christianity
which puts back its own ideas and beliefs into the lips of
Jesus. Fascher sums up the tendencies of the book well
when he writes: 'The late and creative community is at
work; it transforms everything into myth' (*F.M.* 144).

Bultmann has Barthian sympathies, and the publica-
tion of his book, *Jesus*, in 1925, led some to think that
he had modified his radical views since he now uses sayings of Jesus as material for a historical treatment of His
message and significance. In this book 'community-
sayings' often become a transparent veil. Bultmann
will point out how characteristic they are, and that they
could never have been formed if Jesus had not taught
this or that. The procedure of the community, he argues, 'is the best witness for the teaching of Jesus' (*J.*
72). The certainty with which the community put the
eschatological message into His lips is hard to understand if He did not actually proclaim it, and one cannot
doubt that the most important words which demand
complete obedience to God's will go back to Him. The
book did us the service of showing what ought perhaps
not to have been doubted, that a 'community-saying' is
not an invention *ex nihilo*, but a construction which
could not have existed apart from the movement created

by Jesus Himself. Any idea that Bultmann had changed his views has received its quietus in the second edition of *Die Geschichte der synoptischen Tradition* which appeared recently (1931). The book has now grown to 400 pages and is a restatement of the argument with additional matter and comments on subsequent developments. Bultmann's method of answering objections is to restate his original thesis; it is very much as if he observed: 'But did you hear what I said? Let me put it again'. It would not be unfair to describe the work as a study in the cult of the conceivable. But I believe that no small part of his 'scepticism' is the painful anxiety of the trained investigator in no way to fail in doing full justice to the formative activity of any community which appeals, and must appeal, to the words of a revered Teacher. The real charge against him is that he is kinder to the possibilities than to the probabilities of things.

The next writer to whom I must refer is M. Albertz. His *Die synoptischen Streitgespräche* was almost ready for printing in 1918, but owing to the difficulties of the German learned press at that time it was not published until 1921; and it was during the interval that successively the works of Dibelius, Schmidt, and Bultmann came into his hands. It is therefore with truth that he says that the ideas of *Formgeschichte* were 'in the air'. The book contains only part of his material; it treats the short 'debates' which culminate in a saying of Jesus: but enough is given to reveal the insight and sound critical judgment of the author. Albertz condemns what he calls the 'brazen scepticism' of Bultmann and the literary

interests with which, in his opinion, it is too closely associated.   His own purpose, he explains, is to trace the
final literary products in the Gospels to the actual verbal
contests of Jesus and the oldest community with their
opponents.   A special feature is the success with which
he shows that small collections of 'conflict-stories' must
have existed before Mark was written, and which can
still be found in Mk. ii. 1–iii. 6 and xi. 15–xii. 40.   His
standpoint is well illustrated by his estimate of the
Temptation story: it is the work of an artist, Albertz
contends, but the artist 'is to be sought in Jesus Himself' (*S.S.* 48).

Albertz' work was followed in 1922 by that of G.
Bertram, *Die Leidensgeschichte Jesu und der Christuskult.*
In this book Bertram argues that the Passion-narratives
have attained their present form under the influence of
cult-interests.   But the *Kultus* is interpreted in a peculiar sense.   By this term Bertram means neither the worship of the community nor definite religious festivals,
but 'the inner relation of the believers to the Cult-Hero',
and especially reverence for Jesus arising out of experiences connected with the Resurrection.   He does not
trace the gradual darkening of an original historical
tradition by dogmatic tendencies, but thinks rather of
the records as distilled out of primitive religious experiences.   Believers worship the exalted Lord, and the
heavenly glory which shines around Him is naively reflected back into the story of the earthly life!   As may
be supposed, the critical results of this method are
radical in the extreme; of the historical little or nothing
is left.

It is not every critical school which gains its historian in five years. This was the good fortune of the Form-critical School in 1924 when E. Fascher published his interesting and valuable work, *Die formgeschichtliche Methode*. Fascher's criticisms of the exponents of *Formgeschichte* are searching. The excessive scepticism of Bultmann and Bertram is condemned, but full justice is done to Bultmann's analytical skill. Dibelius hardly receives the sympathetic appraisal his work deserves. Doubtless his attempt to trace different classes of material to preachers, narrators, and teachers, calls for criticism; but to ask for the renunciation of the 'constructive method' is not warranted. Form-Criticism will prove a dull and fruitless enterprise if constructive suggestions are barred, and the plea that it must tread the sober path of analytic and literary criticism comes perilously near the demand that it must abandon imagination in the pursuit of its goal. Nor must it be forgotten that Bultmann, praised by Fascher for his neglect of the 'constructive method', follows this very path, as Dibelius has reminded us (*T.R.* 1929, p. 194), since he assumes the existence of 'community-debates' out of which 'ideal scenes' and sayings of Jesus took their rise. Albertz emerges best out of Fascher's hands. He is praised because he has understood how to point the way from the living discourse to the fixed literary form. In the last part of his book Fascher discusses the terminology of the new school and the burning question of the relation of form to history. He expresses astonishment that Dibelius and Bultmann look for the *Sitz im Leben* in the community and not in Jesus Himself, and goes so far as to say

B

that 'the form alone permits no historical value-judgments' (*F.M.* 223). Fascher's attitude, it will be seen, is one of caution. He thinks that the historian will take up Form-Criticism as a new and finer instrument, but that it remains his instrument, one among many. The primary considerations are historical, and to these factors those relating to form must subordinate themselves (*F.M.* 228). This is very much the attitude of B. S. Easton, who thinks that Form-Criticism as a historical tool 'has a very limited utility', but that it may prepare the way for historical criticism (*G.G.* 81).

There is no need that I should treat in detail the subsequent discussions to which Form-Criticism has given rise in Germany, Great Britain, France, Holland, and the United States. L. Brun (*Die Auferstehung Christi*, 1925) has subjected the Resurrection narratives to a penetrating analysis, and P. Fiebig (*Der Erzählungsstil der Evangelien*, 1925) has published an invaluable book in which he examines the narrative style of the Gospels and compares it with that of the sayings, stories, and parables of the Rabbinic tradition. K. L. Schmidt (*Die Stellung der Evangelien in der allgemeinen Literaturgeschichte*, an essay in *Eucharisterion für Gunkel*), had already in 1923 discussed the place of the Gospels as popular cult-books in the history of literature, and in the same collection H. Windisch examined the narrative style of the Fourth Gospel (*Der Johanneische Erzählungsstil*). Many learned essays have also been contributed, notably by M. Goguel, H. J. Cadbury, and O. Cullmann. Three pamphlets deserve special mention: Bultmann's *Die Erforschung der synoptischen Evangelien*,

1925; Dibelius' essay, *Zur Formgeschichte der Evangelien*, in the *Theologische Rundschau*, 1929; and L. Koehler's *Das formgeschichtliche Problem des N.T.*, 1927. Bultmann's essay is just a summary of his larger work. Dibelius replies to criticisms, and shows a readiness to extend the concept of preaching so as to include teaching and discussions within the community. Koehler's essay is largely hostile. 'The problem of the New Testament', he says, 'is not a form-critical, but a historical-critical problem' (*F.P.* 41). It would not be right to end this survey without a reference to C. F. Burney's book, *The Poetry of our Lord*, 1925, which, if not a *formgeschichtliche* investigation, treats in an illuminating way many of the phenomena of form and structure which meet us in the sayings and discourses of Jesus.

III

The historical sketch will have served the purpose, I hope, not only of introducing the leading members of the Form-critical School, but also of indicating some of the main problems with which they are concerned. I must reserve a fuller account of these problems, and of the methods adopted, for the next lecture when the formative process in general will be described. But even at the present stage some preliminary estimate of the value of Form-Criticism must be attempted and of the relation in which it stands to earlier methods of study. It is surely a mistake to regard Form-Criticism as an alternative to Literary and Historical Criticism. Perhaps the Form-Critics would not contest this, but often they appear to proceed as if they had lighted upon a

method which supersedes all others. They rest too
lightly on the results of Source-Criticism, and, without
adequately acknowledging the fact, are compelled again
and again to have recourse to principles which belong to
the study of historical tradition in general. This, in itself, is enough to show that Form-Criticism has decided
limitations, and we shall see that it is further limited
when material is encountered which has no distinctive
form. Moreover, assumptions are constantly made
which, to say the least, demand scrutiny, such as the too
confident belief that the primitive tradition consisted
almost entirely of isolated units and was purely popular
in origin.

But having said this I hasten to add that I have no
doubt that the value of Form-Criticism is considerable.
Fascher's excellent simile of a fine tool which has its limitations may easily foster a neglect which cannot be justified. 'A tool with limited powers!' one may say in
a tone of depreciation. But a tool is something to be
used, whatever its limitations may be. Form-Criticism
is not an instrument by which we can solve the problems
of Gospel Origins, but it can play its part in that task.
It will break in our hands if we use it for ends for which
it was never intended; for other purposes it cannot be
bettered. It has certainly succeeded in pointing out
definite narrative-forms which meet us in popular tradition, and has made important suggestions regarding the
life-story of these and the causes which gave them shape.
But its most valuable service is that it helps us to penetrate the hinterland of the decades from 30 to 50 A.D.
and place ourselves in imagination among the young

Palestinian communities, so that we can enter the 'twilight period' and, in the words of A. Meyer, 'are permitted still to be earwitnesses, to hear the disciples of Jesus and through them Jesus Himself' (*E.M.* 54). Nor is it merely a matter of recovering lost pages of Church History, for we can compare the results we reach with the inferences suggested by Source-Criticism, and thus more surely ground our estimates of the historical beginnings of Christianity.   It is a mistake to suppose that Form-Criticism necessarily leads to scepticism, for this result is reached only by ignoring the limits of the method and by using historical assumptions which vitiate the inquiry from the beginning.   Form-Criticism is a key to some of the doors which hide the Gospel tradition in its formative period: for other doors we require other keys; and for some we have no keys at all.   The present lectures are an attempt to use some of these keys in the belief that the task of our generation is a renewed, untiring investigation of the problems of Gospel Origins.   Of this task we may truly say what Harnack said of Source-Criticism: it is one which 'involves real scavenger's labour in which one is almost choked with dust'.[1]   But if this is so, it is also true that there are pearls in the dust, and that no one can honestly work without finding some of them.

[1]Cf. *The Sayings of Jesus*, xii.

II

THE FORMATIVE PROCESS IN THE
PRIMITIVE COMMUNITIES

IN the present lecture we shall consider the formative process in the first Christian communities, the methods by which it may be studied, and the circumstances which determined its character. Since these are the questions which the Form-Critics more than others have investigated, it will be well to begin by describing their methods and by subjecting them to criticism.

I

1. The first task of Form-Criticism is to *classify* the Synoptic material according to its form. For this purpose it does not matter whether a narrative or a saying comes from Mark, Q, or any other source which critics have posited, since the object of study is the primitive tradition before it was committed to writing. The Fourth Gospel offers a much less promising field, because the material in that Gospel has more obviously passed through a process of development in which Christian experience and literary purposes have played their part.

(*a*) The fundamental distinction in the Synoptic material is that between the narratives and the sayings; but among the narratives there are stories which stand much nearer to the discourse-tradition than to the narrative-tradition proper. From the standpoint of form, the main characteristic of these stories is that they quickly reach their climax in a saying of Jesus which was of interest to the first Christians because it bore directly upon questions of faith and practice. In isolating the stories there is a considerable measure of agreement, independently reached, between Dibelius, Bultmann, and Albertz.[1] In these stories only a sparing use of detail is made; no portraiture of persons is attempted, and of the situation only enough is indicated to make the account intelligible. Usually a question is put to Jesus by enemies or friends, or a query is prompted by an act of healing or an incident. To the question Jesus replies, sometimes by means of a counter-question, at other times by a pointed ethical or religious precept; and with His word the story ends, although a statement may be added which indicates the effect produced on the hearers or the crowd.   Mk. ii. 16f. and Lk. xii. 13-5 are typical examples.

'And the scribes of the Pharisees, when they saw that he was eating with the sinners and publicans, said unto his disciples, "He eateth with publicans and sinners".   And when Jesus heard it, he saith unto them, "They that are whole have no need of a physician, but they that are sick: I came not to call the righteous, but sinners".'

'And one out of the multitude said unto him, "Master, bid my brother divide the inheritance with me".   But he said unto him, "Man, who made me a judge or a divider over you?"   And he

[1]It is right, however, to say that earlier scholars, P. Wendling and H. von Soden, had already pointed out the stylistic differences between the conflict-scenes of Mk. ii. 1–iii. 6 and the miracle-stories of Mk. iv. 35–v. 43.

said unto them, "Take heed, and keep yourselves from all covet-
ousness: for a man's life consisteth not in the abundance of the
things which he possesseth".'

Dibelius calls these short stories *Paradigmen* ('models')
because he believes that they owe their form to the fact
that they were used in sermons as illustrations. This
term is determined by his 'constructive method'. Bultmann uses the name *Apophthegmata*, a term which is
used to describe similar stories in Greek literature; and
with characteristic thoroughness he distinguishes three
types, according as the dialogue is introduced by enemies (*Streitgespräche*), or by friendly inquirers (*Schulgespräche*), or by an incident (*biographischen Apophthegmata*). Albertz treats *Streitgespräche* only.

(*b*) Both Dibelius and Bultmann point out a second
form which appears in some of the longer stories, and
especially in those which record miracles. In these
stories the circumstances are more broadly portrayed
and more detail is introduced. Often the account of a
miracle has three well-marked stages. First, the sufferer is introduced, with some description of his malady
and perhaps a reference to attempts which have failed to
cure him. Then, the cure is described, with greater or
less detail as the case may be, and occasionally with some
account of the means employed. Finally, though this
stage is not always present, the results confirming the
cure are depicted; the demoniac is seen clothed and in
his right mind; the paralytic takes up his bed and walks;
food is ordered for the restored daughter. For these
stories Dibelius uses the name *Novellen* ('tales', 'stories').
Here again his terminology is influenced by his 'con-

structive method'; he believes that in primitive Christianity there existed a class of story-tellers whose delight it was to tell stories which in certain cases might also serve as models for Christian exorcists and healers. Bultmann's term is *Wundergeschichten* ('miracle-stories').

(*c*) The third group contains the sayings of Jesus. Dibelius does not treat these in detail but uses the term *Paränese* ('persuasion', 'exhortation') as a descriptive name, in the belief that the sayings were collected for parenetic or hortatory purposes. Bultmann distinguishes five sub-classes: (1) Logia or Wisdom-words, (2) Prophetic and Apocalyptic words, (3) Law-words and Community-rules, (4) 'I-words',[1] and (5) Parables. All the sayings, wherever they are found, are brought under these categories. The Logia are further treated according to their external features, *i.e.* as similitudes, paradoxes, hyperboles, and examples of parallelism, and according to their constitutive form, *i.e.* as principles, words of exhortation, and questions.

(*d*) The remaining material is that which most of all presents difficulties to the Form-Critic—the stories about Jesus. For these narratives, or for such of them as he treats, Dibelius uses the term *Mythen*, by which he means narratives which explain a rite or the origin of cosmic phenomena, or describe the actions of a divine being. For his examples he cites the stories of the Baptism, the Transfiguration, and the Resurrection. When treating the same material Bultmann's title is *Geschichtserzählung und Legende*. As 'Legends' he includes such narratives as the Activity of the Baptist,

---

[1] *i.e.* sayings in the first person singular.

the Baptism, the Temptation, the Transfiguration, the
Entry into Jerusalem, most of the Passion stories, the
Resurrection narratives, and the Birth Stories of
Matthew and Luke.

Already it will be seen that several important points
arise for discussion and criticism; but it will be best to
postpone these until the remaining stages in the Form-
critical method are described.

2. After classification, the next step is to try to recover the *original form* of the material during the oral
period, and to trace, if possible, the subsequent changes
it has undergone. Justification for this attempt is
claimed on several grounds. In the first place, the
Acts, the Pauline Epistles, and the Epistle of James
supply material for inferences regarding the conditions
of the primitive period. We catch glimpses of the first
Christian assemblies (I. Cor. xi. 18ff., Jas. ii. 1ff.) and hear
echoes of the early preaching (Acts iii. 11ff., I. Cor. xv.
1ff.). Again, the modifications which the later Synoptists make in their sources furnish grounds for inferring
the kind of changes for which we must make allowance
in Mark and Q. 'Laws of the tradition' can be suspected, even if they cannot be laid down as hard and fast
rules, and further evidence of changes is supplied by the
textual tradition and the Apocryphal Gospels. Thirdly,
Rabbinical tradition is available, and evidence can be
obtained from the popular stories and sayings which are
preserved in Greek literature and in the songs and folk-
tales of all lands. The Synoptic material can be compared with parallel matter, and inferences, however peri-
lous they may sometimes be, are made possible. In these

ways it is often possible to work back to a form which
preceded that now found in the Gospels, and which for
various reasons has been modified by the Evangelists.

3. The third task of Form-Criticism is to seek for the
Sitz im Leben, the life-situation, out of which the material springs.   Dibelius, as I have previously said, looks
to preaching for this.   He even states the principle that
the nearer a narrative stands to the sermon, the less it is
under the suspicion of alterations by legendary and
literary influences (*F.E.* 30f.).   This estimate ascribes a
higher protective value to the sermon than many of us
would be prepared to concede, but none the less Dibelius
is right in stressing the formative value of preaching and
its power to awaken latent recollections of actions and
sayings of Jesus.   In his essay of 1929 he reaffirms his
view, and writes: 'The connexion of an essential part of
the tradition about Jesus with preaching appears to me
an assured assumption of all further discussions' (*T.R.*
192).   Albertz thinks that the tradition took shape in
the early Christian assemblies where individual Christians had the right to bring forward narratives for the
strengthening and instruction of their fellow-members.
'If', he says, 'we want to make for ourselves a vivid picture of the teachers of primitive Christianity, we must
not forget these narrators who understood how to serve
in the meetings the growing apologetic interests of the
members of the community by the presentation of appo-
site words of the Lord' (*S.S.* 101).   Schmidt takes a
similar view.   'When the Christians were together,
they narrated one to another concerning the words and
deeds of the Lord, one relieving, one supplementing

another' (*R.G.J.* 19).   Bultmann thinks rather of 'debates' within the Palestinian communities like those which took place in Rabbinic circles in the early centuries of our era.   In these 'debates' the tradition was shaped under the influence of apologetic, polemical, and dogmatic needs.   Words of Jesus were given a narrative framework which, in his opinion, is ideal in character.   The *Apophthegmata*, he holds, are 'ideal constructions'; they are 'not reports about historical events, but constructions which give pictorial expression in a concrete scene to an idea' (*G.S.T.* 40).   He is ready to allow that Jesus healed on the Sabbath or used this or that word in a dispute with an opponent, but for him such questions are beside the point, since his main concern is with the literary character and origin of the *Apophthegmata*.   These, he maintains, are 'ideal scenes which illustrate in a concrete case a principle which the community traces back to Jesus' (*G.S.T.* 41).   He believes that for the most part the formative process took place in the Palestinian communities, but that the miracle-stories and the 'legends' took shape in Hellenistic circles.   His treatment of the discourse-tradition is only less radical.   Here again much is traced to 'community-debates' sometimes in Palestine, and sometimes, as in the case of the 'I-words', in the Hellenistic world.   For the parables he lays down the principle that the best criterion of genuineness is the presence of an opposition to Jewish morality and piety or of the eschatological attitude which characterized the preaching of Jesus, always providing that no specifically Christian details are present (*G.S.T.* 222).

II

However provocative an account of the methods of Form-Criticism may be, it has the merit of bringing before our attention in a challenging way matters which need to be taken into consideration in studying the formation of the Gospel tradition. I propose now to examine some of these points more closely.

1. The first question is whether any definite oral forms existed in primitive Christianity and whether the Form-Critics have succeeded in isolating them. We shall find that this question is inevitably bound up with the problems of terminology.

(a) It may be justly claimed, I think, that the short stories which Dibelius calls *Paradigmen* and Bultmann *Apophthegmata* are actual narrative-forms in which oral tradition naturally clothes itself. Not only have the stories definite formal and stylistic features, they are also closely paralleled in the Rabbinic tradition. As an example I will cite a story given by P. Fiebig (*E.E.* 102).

'An incident concerning a non-Jew who came before Shammai. He said to him: "Make me a proselyte under the condition that thou teachest me the whole Torah while I stand on one leg". Thereupon he repulsed him with a rod which he had in his hand. He came before Hillel. He made him a proselyte. He said to him: "What thou hatest do not to thy neighbour. This is the whole Torah, and all else is its interpretation. Go, learn".'

It will be seen that this story reaches its climax in the words of Hillel, and that to these everything else is subordinated. We do not learn the Gentile's name, or

when or where he came. All that we are told is that he
puts his question to the rival teachers and receives his
answer, and it is obvious that the story was circulated for
the sake of this answer; it crystallized a principle precious to those to whom it was told. There are about
thirty or forty of these stories in the Synoptic Gospels,
and there can be little doubt that in them we have
stories which were told and retold in the first Christian
assemblies. I suggest that neither of the names by
which Dibelius and Bultmann designate the stories is
satisfactory. *Paradigmen* ('models') is too general and
is too exclusively associated with the theory that the
stories were formed under the influence of preaching.
On the other hand, *Apophthegmata* is literary rather than
popular and, by concentrating attention too much on
the final word of Jesus, it almost invites a depreciatory
attitude to the narrative element. For these reasons I
should like to suggest a name which has not yet been
used. Why not call these narratives *Pronouncement-
Stories*? The advantages of the name are that it leaves
the possibilities of origin open; it easily covers the various types; and it emphasizes the main element—a pronouncement, or word of Jesus, bearing on some aspect
of life, belief, or conduct.

(*b*) Among the longer stories there is good reason to
assume the existence of the second popular narrative-
form which consists normally of three stages, an introduction, the account of a cure, and a reference to the
sequel. Here again Dibelius' term *Novellen* is too
general and suffers from its association with the suggestion of an otherwise unknown class of story-tellers in the

first communities. Since the stories of this type usually record the 'mighty works' of Jesus, it is better to adopt Bultmann's term, *Miracle-Stories*, although it must be admitted that the name describes the contents of these stories rather than their constitutive form.

(*c*) For the sayings of Jesus Bultmann's five-fold classification is useful, but here we discover the limitations of Form-Criticism; for the terms do little more than describe stylistic features; they do not denote popular forms into which an individual or a community unconsciously throws sayings. 'What *form* difference is there', B. S. Easton asks, 'between the "logion"— "Whosoever exalteth himself shall be humbled"—the "apocalyptic word"—"Whosoever shall be ashamed of me, the Son of man shall be ashamed of him"—and the "church rule"—"Whosoever putteth away his wife and marrieth another committeth adultery"?' (*G.G.* 74). We may certainly to advantage study the formal aspects of sayings, but when we try to classify them according to popular forms, the attempt breaks down. Moreover, the method is almost bound to result in scepticism. In dealing with popular forms it is natural to stress the activity of a community, and, while this cannot be ignored even in relation to the sayings-tradition, the tendency is to ignore the creative activity of the original speaker. This danger might perhaps be avoided by a Form-Criticism conscious of its limitations, but at present this is a great deal to expect!

(*d*) When we come to the stories about Jesus we reach material which has no definite structural form, and in consequence material in the study of which Form-

Criticism has no power to help us.   This, I think, is
partly indicated by its failure to devise an adequate terminology, and still more by the terminology it adopts.
'Myths' and 'Legends' are terms which do not define
any particular structural forms.   Fascher has justly
pointed out how 'elastic' (*kautschukartig*) the term
'Legend' is.   According to Dibelius it denotes a narrative where the composition is less tense and a heightened
interest is given to persons other than Jesus (cf. *F.E.* 26;
*F.M.*204).   In such narratives 'we stand before the beginnings of Christian legend' (*F.E.* 26).   According to
Bultmann, 'legends' are distinguished by the fact that
their point is the relation in which they stand to the life
of Jesus or to the faith and *Kultus* of the community
(*G.S.T.* 260).   These are certainly formal characteristics, but they are so broad that they fail to indicate any
particular narrative form to which they can apply.   The
term, indeed, has no distinctive meaning until we give it
a definitely historical reference.   In this respect, it is
useless to try to return to an earlier usage; for our time,
'legends' are not *legenda*, narratives about 'famous men'
read for purposes of edification.   To-day, for good or
ill, the term expresses a historical judgment, and an unfavourable judgment.   This is at once apparent in Bultmann's definition.   'As legends', he says, 'I designate
the narrative pieces of the tradition which are not pro-
perly speaking miracle-stories, but which nevertheless
have no historical but a religious and edifying character'
(*G.S.T.* 260).   Here we see at once that 'legend' is not
a formal term; it is a historical label informing us that
the contents are not guaranteed.

2. The criticisms just offered will naturally affect our estimate of the value of Form-Criticism in enabling us to recover the original forms in which the tradition circulated and the life-situation out of which they sprang. We shall expect more from the Pronouncement- and Miracle-Stories than from the rest of the tradition; but in all cases the determining considerations will be historical rather than purely formal. The justification offered for the attempt to reach oral forms has much force. With the Gospels before us we certainly can mark the kind of changes which later Evangelists have made in their sources, and it is right to ask if the same changes have not been effected earlier. The tendency to add names and to sharpen references to statements of time and place are cases in point. But this must not be done in a mechanical manner and without regard to the special characteristics of the individual Evangelists; we cannot assume that Mark would act just as Matthew and Luke have acted. We may speak of 'laws of the tradition' if by these we mean ways in which the minds of those who handed down the tradition had a tendency to act; but we cannot treat these laws as if they described the work of machines, for there is always an 'unknown quantity' in the actions of men which defies calculation. It is right to regard loosely connected sayings like those on Patches and Wineskins (Mk. ii. 21f.) as additions to the Pronouncement-Story on Fasting (Mk. ii. 18-20). In the same way sayings about the Sabbath have been added to the Cornfields story (Mk. ii. 23-6), while a section like Mk. vii. 1-23 (Clean and Unclean) is clearly a compilation of traditional material. But

c

when the attempt is made to disintegrate a Pronouncement-Story, and to distinguish between earlier and later
elements, we are obviously on very speculative ground.
The Fasting story, to which I have just referred, will
serve as an illustration.   Form-Critics of all schools tell
us that in its oral form the story ended with the words of
Mk. ii. 19*a*: 'Can the sons of the bride-chamber fast,
while the bridegroom is with them?'   Here, it is said,
the original oral form reached its climax.   The first
Christians defended their abstention from Jewish fasts
by quoting the reply of Jesus when He was challenged
regarding His disciples; His words were their charter of
freedom.   But in the story as we have it in Mark, the
question is followed by the words: 'As long as they have
the bridegroom with them, they cannot fast.   But the
days will come, when the bridegroom shall be taken
away from them, and then will they fast in that day' (Mk.
ii. 19*b*-20).   This, say the Form-Critics, is not the
word of Jesus; it is a 'community-product'.   The later
Christian community has departed from an earlier attitude of freedom, and it justifies its practice by putting
back into the lips of Jesus a prophecy which adapts His
words to the existing situation.   Now this explanation
may be true; but it transcends any principles belonging
to form, and is really a study in historical probability.
I should prefer to describe it as a study in historical im-
probability.   It overstresses the undoubted freedom of
Jesus and His disciples in respect of Jewish ritual practices; for the words: 'When ye fast, be not, as the hypo-
crites, of a sad countenance' (Mt. vi. 16) show that
Jesus made no decisive breach with Jewish customs,

while the alleged change on the part of the first Christians from a liberal to a conservative attitude reverses the actual process visible in such matters as circumcision and the question of eating with Gentiles. Moreover, the explanation passes too lightly over the question how the words of Jesus could be so neatly transformed into a composite utterance which combines a historical report with something which Jesus never said. One feels that the ingenuity of a suggestion which commends itself even to the prudent Albertz (*S.S.* 9) has been too easily accepted by many who repeat it as something hardly to be questioned.

This example has been considered in some detail in order to show that caution is necessary in separating editorial supplements and traditional accretions from primitive oral forms. The attempt itself is commendable, and in cases like those I have mentioned can be carried out with results which elucidate the story of the formation of the tradition. Naturally, inferences of this kind are strengthened when they are reached by different investigators working independently, but in all cases they should be subjected to continual review.

3. With similar qualifications, justification can also be claimed for the attempt to ascertain the *Sitz im Leben*, the life-situation, of the primitive oral forms. The scope afforded for subjective treatment in this field is obvious, but it would be unjust to the Form-Critics to describe their work as imagination at leisure. Imagination has its legitimate rights in historical research, provided it is controlled by sound methods and by an ade-

quate number of available facts.   The chief danger to be avoided is that of limiting the life-situation unduly by emphasizing too strongly any one of the controlling factors, such as the influence of preaching.   Every consideration bearing on the life of the first Christians must be taken into account—the practical demands arising from daily life, the need to explain the new faith to themselves and to others, the necessities of defence against objections and slanders from unfriendly and hostile neighbours.   These and other considerations have determined the form which the tradition now has, and the changes it has undergone, and by taking them into account it is often possible to explain why this or that element in the tradition has survived and why much we should greatly desire to know has not been handed down to us.

All the Form-Critics rightly emphasize the social aspects of the formative process.   Little has survived which springs from the caprice of individuals or which is interesting merely in and for itself.   For this reason the Form-Critics are right in urging the importance of the meetings of the community as the area in which the tradition developed, and also in stressing the influence of the religious life of the first Christians as expressed in worship.   On the other hand, Bultmann's theory of 'community-debates' carries a sound principle to impossible lengths.   It is to this criticism that Fascher devotes some of his liveliest pages.   Bultmann, he says, 'seeks the *Sitz im Leben* almost exclusively in the primitive community and diverts attention from the life of Jesus so that the question, whether the form is perhaps

only a reproduction of living actuality, is not even put.
All is a production of the primitive community according to the recipe "Situation + Logion = Apophthegma"'
(*F.M.* 223). He is right in claiming that 'the Straus-
sian scepticism is operative here, the opinion that
"ideas" are true even though they have not gained a historical existence' (*ib.*). Moreover, the term 'community-debates' is misleading. We know that such debates
took place among the Jews in the early centuries of our
era when the Rabbinic tradition took definite form, but
it is only with serious qualifications that we can use this
analogy when we think of the first Christians. If in
Corinth there were 'not many mighty, not many noble',
still more must this have been true of Palestine. The
first Christian assemblies must have been gatherings of
poor men, afire with great hopes, but marked by little intellectual skill or argumentative ability, and it was in the
Providence of God that it was so. For this reason the
learned debates at Jamnia are a delusive analogy, and it
is better to picture the conditions more broadly. We
must think of a time when recollections of the words and
deeds of Jesus were both living and latent. So far as
they were latent, they were stirred into life by the various
needs I have described. Problems relating to the Sabbath, fasting, marriage, taxation; thoughts about the
Cross and the Resurrection; inquiries about Jesus and
objections to His message; all these would kindle recollection and prompt the relating of His words and deeds
in the first assemblies. If at times an ideal element
entered into the tradition, if circumstances were misun-
derstood and words of His were coloured by thoughts

precious to the narrators, what is this beyond that which
we might reasonably expect?   The extent to which this
is the case is obviously a matter for serious consideration, but a reconstruction which implies the untrust-
worthiness of the greater part of the tradition is wanting
in probability and is not just to the Gospel records.

III

It remains for us to consider the fundamental assumption of Form-Criticism, that, in the main, the
earliest tradition consisted of small isolated units without local or temporal connexions; and further, since the
two questions are inseparable, to ask what place is to be
given to the recollections of eyewitnesses.   With the
Gospel of Mark before us it is impossible to deny that
the earliest tradition was largely a mass of fragments.
Stories like the Call of the First Disciples (Mk. i. 16-20)
and the Healing of a Leper (Mk. i. 40-5) are not only
self-contained but are the despair of those who make a
serious attempt to narrate the life of Jesus; and the same
is true of the Appointment of the Twelve (Mk. iii. 13-9),
the Beelzebub Controversy (Mk. iii. 22-6), the Teaching
by the Lake (Mk. iv. 1ff.), and many other sections.   In
longer passages like Mk. ii. 1–iii. 6 and xi. 15–xii. 40
the arrangement is plainly topical and points to a time
when the ten stories in question circulated separately.
Moreover, the same features reappear in the special
tradition of Matthew and Luke, while the temporal and
local statements which the later Evangelists introduce
into their Markan material are prompted less by outside
information than by inferences based on the material

itself.   The basal assumption of *Formgeschichte* appears
then to be fully justified.

On the other hand, we have already seen that several
of the Form-Critics modify this assumption to the extent of recognizing in the Passion Story an early continuous narrative, and that Albertz traces the two collections of Pronouncement-Stories in Mk. ii. 1–iii. 6 and
xi. 15–xii. 40 to a comparatively early time.   These,
however, are not the only modifications which the facts
compel us to make.   The four stories of Mk. i. 21-39
form a historical unity.   After the incident in the synagogue Jesus enters the house of Simon and Andrew; in
the evening crowds gather at the door and many healings
take place; while the following morning 'a great while
before day' He goes into a desert place and resists the
entreaties of those who urge Him to return to Capernaum.   Such a closely articulated sequence obviously
demands explanation, and the need is all the greater if
anything like Schmidt's simile of a heap of unstrung
pearls describes Mark's material (*R.G.J.* 281).   Nor is
this the only example of the kind: the series of miracle-
stories in Mk. iv. 35-v. 43 has the framework of an
itinerary.   It is true that the temporal indications are
defective: the journey begins in the late afternoon (iv.
35), and apparently everything, including the Jaïrus
story, happens on the same day.   But, at most, this is
a sign of the narrator's limitations; it does not destroy
the cohesion of the series.   Indeed, the principal difficulty Schmidt raises is the rather desperate suggestion
that εἰς τὸ πέραν is a kind of technical expression
which always refers to the *east* or *north-east* side of the

lake, and that therefore originally the Jaïrus incident must have been located on that side (*R.G.J.* 145). Again, fragments of another journey are visible in Mk. vi. 31–viii. 26.   If critical opinion is right in finding here a doublet in which the same journey is described twice over (cf. vi. 31–vii. 37 and viii. 1-26), there is added reason for realizing how deeply the tradition of a meal followed by a crossing of the lake and a controversy with the Pharisees was embedded in primitive Christian recollection.   Schmidt justly observes that 'an author who had of himself formed these stories would have brought about a simpler and more consecutive topography', and that a tradition of this kind 'has special value for the historian' (*R.G.J.* 209).

But besides considerations of this kind there is in the Story of the Ministry, as Mark gives it, a sense of movement which is even more impressive when attention has been drawn to the many gaps in the outline.   Mark's Gospel is no formless collection.   A central place is given to the great day at Caesarea Philippi, when Jesus asks: 'Who say ye that I am?' (Mk. viii. 29), and it cannot be accidental that, while before this incident there are only two references to the 'Son of man' (Mk. ii. 10, 28), no less than twelve follow it.   The Transfiguration six days later (ix. 2) is dated with precision, and a period of instruction is followed by the account, admittedly fragmentary, of the Last Journey to Jerusalem (x. 32ff.). These are some of the features which in the past have led critics of all schools to suppose that Mark had access to good tradition concerning the Public Ministry of Jesus. At the moment it is the fashion to minimize these points, to dwell on the gaps in the outline, and to describe Mark as a collector of scattered traditions; but there can be little doubt that this is a passing phase, and that a sounder criticism will return to the earlier view, with the recognition, however, that the outline is less complete than had been supposed.[1]   All this opens up the interesting question as to how far the formation of the primitive tradition was influenced by 'eyewitnesses and ministers of the word'.

It is on this question of eyewitnesses that Form-Criticism presents a very vulnerable front.   If the Form-Critics are right, the disciples must have been translated to heaven immediately after the Resurrection. As Bultmann sees it, the primitive community exists *in vacuo*, cut off from its founders by the walls of an inexplicable ignorance.   Like Robinson Crusoe it must do the best it can.   Unable to turn to any one for information, it must invent situations for the words of Jesus, and put into His lips sayings which personal memory cannot check.   All this is absurd; but there is a reason for this unwillingness to take into account the existence of leaders and eyewitnesses.   Indeed, there are two reasons.   By the very nature of his studies the Form-Critic is not predisposed in favour of eyewitnesses; he deals with oral forms shaped by nameless individuals, and the recognition of persons who could enrich the tradition by their actual recollections comes as a disturbing element to the smooth working of the theory.   He is faced by an unknown quantity just where he wants to operate with

[1]See the excellent article by C. H. Dodd, 'The Framework of the Gospel Narrative', *E.T.* xliii. 396-400.

precise 'laws of the tradition'.   Again, the Form-Critic
knows how greatly the influence of eyewitnesses has
been exaggerated.   Papias tells us that Mark had been
Peter's 'attendant' and that he 'wrote down accurately
all that he remembered of the things done and said by
Christ, but not however in order'.   Too often this has
been interpreted as if everything in Mark's Gospel
could at once be traced back to Peter's testimony.   Ex-
aggerations of this kind bring their own punishment.
The result is that other factors, vital to the understanding of the Gospels, remain hidden; preoccupied with
Peter we fail to allow for the influence of current tradition on Mark.   It is the recognition of this danger
which in a large measure accounts for the neglect of
Papias in much present-day criticism.   The pendulum
swings from one extreme to the other.   But this is as
mistaken as it is natural.   Papias is repeating the words
of an Elder who must have been a younger contemporary of Peter, and the sobriety of the statement is all in
its favour.   However disturbing to the smooth working
of theories the influence of eyewitnesses on the formation of the tradition cannot possibly be ignored.   The
one hundred and twenty at Pentecost did not go into
permanent retreat; for at least a generation they moved
among the young Palestinian communities, and through
preaching and fellowship their recollections were at the
disposal of those who sought information.   Unfortunately, as the material in the Gospel shows, the first
Christians did not possess the biographical interests
which mark the modern man; they neither put, nor
thought of putting questions we should deem of first im-

portance.   Moreover, we have to allow for the gradual disappearance by death of the first witnesses and for the prevailing interest in the speedy Return of Christ.   But when all qualifications have been made, the presence of personal testimony is an element in the formative process which it is folly to ignore.   By its neglect of this factor Form-Criticism gains in internal coherence, but it loses its power to accomplish its main task which is to describe the *Sitz im Leben* of the tradition.

In my presentation of Form-Criticism, it may seem that I have so much to criticize that I ought forthwith to express the opinion that the new method has little to contribute to the understanding of Gospel Origins.   I cannot say this because it would not be true.   I have already accepted several fruitful suggestions from Form-Criticism, and these will be developed in the succeeding lectures.   Further, it is the Form Critics who raise and face the special questions which belong to any serious study of the formative process.   It is of value to discuss unacceptable suggestions if only to be confronted with the necessity of seeking for answers which are better and more satisfying.

III

THE PASSION-NARRATIVES

In the first lecture I mentioned the opinion of Dibelius and Schmidt that the Passion Story was the first part of the primitive tradition to attain the form of a continuous narrative. The same view is held by W. Bussmann, who during the last few years (1925-31) has published a series of detailed Synoptic Studies (cf. *S.Sn.* iii. 177). Among the Form-Critics, Bertram rejects this view; he holds that the Passion-narrative consists of single stories which by degrees grew up into a whole. In this opinion he claims the support of Bultmann, and not without justification (*L.J.C.* 8). We shall see, however, that Bultmann also thinks of a connected Passion Story and that in this respect the difference between the Form-Critics is mainly a matter of degree. The connected story, as Bultmann finds it, is very brief, and he is more ready than Dibelius and Schmidt to recognize the existence of separate stories (*pericopae*) which, by a process of editing, gradually found their way into the narrative as we now know it; but he, no less than these scholars, posits a primitive nucleus of connected stories.

The arguments which support the hypothesis are attractive and forcible. In the first place, the Story as it appears in the Gospels has the nature of a connected his-

torical account more than any other part of the tradition; this, in itself, suggests that the Evangelists had
access to a relatively fixed complex of stories. Again,
apart from differences in certain respects, the Gospels
are in substantial agreement as to the course of events.
Matthew's version is simply a second edition of Mark's
account with additions which are secondary in value
and importance. In Luke's version the deviations are
more striking, but they are subordinate to a general
similarity of plan, and this is true also of the Fourth Gospel where religious and doctrinal interests are more obviously present. This similarity of structure is naturally explained if the tradition was continuous from the
beginning. Further, the nature of the record points in
the same direction: the course of events is convincingly
portrayed, and, while difficulties arise in several points,
the narrative as a whole is marked by a realism and a
sobriety of tone which leave on the mind a good impression of its historical value. How forcible this impression can be appears in the observations which the historian Eduard Meyer has made in the first part of his
Ursprung und Anfänge des Christentums (5th ed. 1924).
Of the tradition of the Last Supper he says that 'it belongs to the oldest constituent elements in the Gospel'
(i. 174), that the Gethsemane story and the Arrest go
back mainly to Peter (i. 183), that there can be no doubt
that Jesus acknowledged Himself to be the Messiah in
answer to the high priest's question (i. 194). Of the
narratives leading up to the Passion in Mk. xii. he says:
'All these narratives are so vivid and living and corre-
spond so completely to the situation that there can be no

doubt that they go back to the best tradition, and in all
that is essential are authentic' (i. 166). Schmidt draws
attention to the silence of Jesus in the Passion Story.
'While elsewhere Jesus conducts long polemical debates
with His opponents, in the account of the Passion He is
almost silent' (*R.G.J.* 305). He argues that, for edifying and religious purposes, a later time would have put
into the mouth of Jesus words addressed to the Sanhedrim, to Pilate, or to Herod. This is not a mere matter
of opinion, as a study of the writings collected by Dr.
M. R. James in his *Apocryphal New Testament* (1924) will
show. In the *Acts of John* the Lord converses with the
Apostle John on the Mount of Olives during the actual
Crucifixion, and explains that though to the multitude
below He is being crucified and pierced with lances and
reeds, He has appeared to him to explain those things
'which it behoveth a disciple to learn from his teacher
and a man from his God' (*A.N.T.* 254). In the *Acts of
Pilate* Jesus replies to the question, 'What is truth?' and
says: 'Truth is of heaven'; and when Pilate asks: 'Is
there not truth upon the earth?' Jesus says: 'Thou seest
how that they which speak the truth are judged of them
that have authority upon earth' (*A.N.T.* 100). In the
Gospel of St. Bartholomew Jesus after His Resurrection
answers many questions, and among other things tells
how He went from the Cross to Hades to bring up
Adam and all with him at the supplication of the arch-
angel Michael. Schmidt is fully justified in arguing
that the Passion Story in the Gospels was preserved
from treatment of this kind because it had already
and for a long time attained a fixed form. He very

finely adds that for the oldest community 'the Story
as it happened was itself apology enough' (*R.G.J.*
306).

But in addition to the points that have been urged
the argument which is most characteristic of the Form-
Critics must be considered: this is the contention that
the situation in which the primitive community found
itself demanded a continuous Passion Story. Almost
from the first the followers of Jesus found themselves
faced by a serious difficulty; both for themselves and
others it was necessary to be able to show how a Crucified Messiah could be the subject of a message of Salvation. The first Christians were not long in discovering
that such a message was 'unto Jews a stumbling-block,
and unto Gentiles foolishness' (I Cor. i. 23). Arguments from Old Testament prophecies were not enough
to meet this difficulty; such arguments made it the more
necessary to tell the Story of the Cross and to tell it as a
whole. 'Here', Dibelius says, 'was the Salvation
visible, not only in the Person and word of the Lord, but
in the course of a series of events' (*F.E.* 12). It was
necessary to tell the connected Story, and 'so much the
more as only the account of the succession of Passion
and Easter solves the paradox of the Cross, only the
combination of the events satisfies the need for interpretation, only the connexion of the individual incidents
can answer the question of guilt (*Schuldfrage*)' (*F.E.*
12). Thus Dibelius maintains that the interests of
edification, of the most primitive theology, and of the
simplest apology combined to make it needful to narrate
the whole Passion Story. In like manner Schmidt

argues that to tell single incidents satisfied the need neither of the narrator, the liturgist, nor the apologist. He points out that many of the narratives have neither religious (*kultische*) nor apologetic power. 'Only in a context in which certain pieces are needed as a preparation for other pieces, is this power perceptible' (*R.G.J.* 305). Accordingly, he concludes that 'in its full extent the Passion Story will have been publicly read in religious worship as a *lectio continua*'. He adds that it is only as a whole that the Story could give an answer to a question which must have emerged again and again in the early missionary-period: 'How could Jesus have been brought to the Cross by the people who were blessed by His signs and wonders?' (*ib.*).

It must be recognized, I think, that in the foregoing arguments the Form-Critics state a strong case. Where this is so it is not desirable to add arguments which are more uncertain; but it may be of interest to examine a contention which has not yet run the gauntlet of critical debate. Bussmann has recently argued that when Paul says that 'Christ died for our sins κατὰ τὰς γραφάς' and that He was raised 'on the third day κατὰ τὰς γραφάς' (I Cor. xv. 3f.), he implies the existence of a written Passion and Resurrection Story (*S.Sn.* iii. 180-91). Bussmann sets aside the commonly accepted view that the phrase refers to the Old Testament, on the ground that none of the passages which have been cited —Psa. xvi. 8-11, Isa. liii. 5, 2 Kings xx. 5, Jon. i. 17 and Hos. vi. 2—can have been meant by Paul. He points out that Paul nowhere else quotes the Old Testament when speaking of Christ's death as a death 'for us', that his usual formula of citation is καθὼς γέγραπται or some equivalent phrase, and that he uses the singular ἡ γραφή when he refers to the Old Testament, except in three cases which are not really exceptions to this rule.[1] Accordingly, he concludes that Paul is appealing, not to the Old Testament, but 'to accounts of the Passion Story existing in the community, perhaps even to one or some of the attempts at Gospel-writings mentioned by Luke' (*S.Sn.* iii. 190).

What is the force of this contention?   It would not be right to argue from I Cor. xv. 3f. alone that in Paul's day a written account of the Passion was in existence. When, however, there are good grounds for thinking that a continuous tradition existed at a very early date, Bussmann's interpretation becomes very persuasive.   If the reference is not to the passages cited above, it becomes necessary, in default of Bussmann's explanation, to interpret Paul's words as a vague reference to the general trend of Old Testament teaching.

An alternative suggestion is that the phrase κατὰ τὰς γραφάς refers to a systematically arranged pre-Pauline collection of Testimonies from the Scriptures, directed in the first place *adversus Judaeos* and then used for building up positive Christian teaching.[2]   In this case, Bussmann's argument falls to the ground, and the exist-

---

[1] In Rom. i. 2 the article is omitted and the adjective 'holy' is added Rom. xvi. 26 is of doubtful authenticity; and in Rom. xv. 4 the phrase 'the writings' may not refer to the Old Testament at all (Bussmann, *S.Sn.* iii. 186f).

[2] Cf. D. Plooij, *Studies in the Testimony Book*, 1932, p. 6f.

D

ence of early Passion-narratives must rest on the arguments already mentioned.

II

Immediately it is recognized that at an early period the events of the Passion were narrated as a continuous narrative, several questions arise in the mind. Was the Story current in several forms? Were separate individual stories gradually incorporated within the continuous records? Why is the thread of continuity so much stronger in the Passion Story than it is in the Resurrection tradition?

Several considerations favour the view that the Passion Story was current in different forms. A single Story, as the foundation of all the Gospel accounts, would imply from the beginning a highly organized Church governed from one centre; an authoritative basis would have been necessary to ensure its sole survival value. It seems more probable that different communities, whenever it was possible, would have had their own accounts. This view is supported by analogies suggested by the sayings-tradition and the history of the Gospel text. The Synoptic data are leading us to think that parallel collections of the words of Jesus were drawn up at different centres, while in later times the existence of local texts, associated with the Great Churches of early Christianity, is becoming the assumption of modern Textual Criticism. The probabilities, then, favour the existence of several Passion Stories; and this view is not ruled out by the fact that the Markan Story, by reason of its merits and its Petrine basis, outstripped others in its influence and the range of its dissemination.

Is this assumption supported by the critical evidence? Arguing from evidence of this kind, Bussmann has recently found reason to presuppose four Passion Stories: two in Mark, a third in the special tradition in Luke and John, and a fourth in the distinctively Matthaean tradition (*S.Sn.* iii. 177). So far as Mark and Matthew are concerned this view seems doubtful; but the evidence distinctly favours the hypothesis in Luke and in John.

In *Behind the Third Gospel* I have argued that fundamentally the Lukan account of the Passion is non-Markan, but that Luke added extracts from Mark which to a considerable extent can still be isolated. In this lecture I can only indicate the main arguments broadly. In the first place, the small percentage of words common to Luke and Mark points to the independence of the Lukan Passion Story. Sir John Hawkins has computed the percentage at 27 as compared with over 50 per cent. in the earlier common sections (*O.S.* 78).

This percentage is low if we allow for the fact that the most diverse accounts would contain words in common like 'crucify', 'betray', and many others; but, further, the 'common words' are curiously distributed: they are not spread evenly over the Lukan account, but appear in verses and half-verses, and, with their removal, the continuity of the Story is often improved. This claim can be tested by examining the following fourteen passages which have been taken from Mark: Lk. xxii. 19*a*, 22, 34, 46*b*(?), 50*b*, 52-3*a*, 54*b*-61; xxiii. 3, 26, 34*b*(?), 38, 44f., 50-4; xxiv. 10 (?). It may be, of course,

that other passages have been taken from Mark; but
since, apart from these passages, the percentage of
'common words' is 19, the gleanings are not likely to be
many.   Now when these Markan passages are removed,
they form a mere heap, while that which is left is a
readable whole, not without gaps, but with a continuity
far greater than we have a right to expect, as I have
shown in my pamphlet, *The First Draft of St. Luke's
Gospel.*[1]

These arguments do not state the whole case. I have
shown, for example, that of the twelve places where the
Lukan order of events in the Passion Story differs from
that of Mark (cf. Sir John Hawkins, *O.S.* 81ff.) no less
than seven are included in my list of 'Markan insertions', and that it is because these insertions have been
made that the variations of order are present. I have
also shown that with a single exception (Lk. xxii. 22),
the fourteen insertions appear in Luke, *relatively to each
other*, in precisely the same succession as in Mark. I
have therefore suggested that Luke first noted them in
Mark, and then transferred them one by one to his own
Passion Story because he wanted to enrich it and make it
more complete.[2]

These arguments are so simple, and so confirmatory
one to another, that the hypothesis of an independent
Lukan Passion Story appears to me to be lifted above
the realms of mere conjecture as much as any source-
hypothesis is ever likely to be.

[1]Published by the S.P.C.K.   The Lukan text of the Revised Version
is given without the passages which come from Mark.

[2]Cf. *B.T.G.* 33-75.

I turn now to the Fourth Gospel. Here the case for an independent Passion Narrative has not received the attention it deserves. I fear, however, that the conditions are such that a clear result will never be possible. Like the other Evangelists, the Fourth Evangelist uses earlier sources, but he puts his own stamp upon everything he uses to such an extent that literary analysis can achieve little in the task of reconstruction. In these circumstances, indications of a special Passion Source are all that we can hope to find. Personally, I believe that the indications exist. The royal manner in which the Evangelist disposes of his material, and neglects so much of that which is contained in Mark, is best explained if he had an independent Story to tell. Moreover, as is well-known, he shares many points of detail with Luke.[1] It is often said that these and other agreements show that John used the Third Gospel. I have always thought that this view is more than the evidence demands, and that the parallels are adequately accounted for if the special Lukan and Johannine traditions overlapped, and so shared elements in common. In any case, the existence of a special Johannine tradition is suggested by many points which are peculiar to the Fourth Gospel. These include the stories of the

[1]John and Luke agree that after Supper Jesus conversed with His disciples, and about service in particular (xiii. 16; Lk. xxii. 26f.); that Satan entered into Judas (xiii. 27; Lk. xxii. 3); that the Denial was foretold before leaving the Supper room (xiii. 36ff.; Lk. xxii. 31ff.); that the Mount of Olives was a favourite resort of Jesus (xviii. 2; Lk. xxii. 39); that the servant lost his right ear (xviii. 10; Lk. xxii. 50); that Pilate pronounced Jesus innocent three times (xviii. 38, xix. 4, 6; Lk. xxiii. 4, 14, 22); that the sepulchre had never been used before (xix. 41; Lk. xxiii. 53).

Feet-washing (xiii. 2-11), Judas and the Beloved Disciple (xiii. 21-30), the Mother of Jesus at the Cross (xix. 25-7), the Piercing of the side (xix. 31-7); the references to Annas, the disciple 'known unto the high priest', the Pavement, the seamless robe (xviii. 13, 16; xix. 13, 23); and, above all, the date of the Supper, which is placed before the Passover (xviii. 28). However impossible it may be to distinguish between the tradition and its form in the Gospel, the evidence suggests that Ephesus had a Passion Story of its own.

So far as Matthew is concerned, there is no evidence that he knew any Passion Story other than that of Mark. 51 per cent. of his words agree wholly or in part with those of Mark, and his additions consist mainly of popular stories which amplify the Markan Narrative, and attempt to answer the questions it raised. The Judas stories (xxvi. 14-6, xxvii. 3-10) throw yet darker shadows on the traitor's deed. The stories of Pilate and his wife (xxvii. 19, 24f.) deepen the horror of the governor's situation. The Earthquake and the Resurrection of the Saints (xxvii. 51b-3) enhance the miraculous element in the mysterious darkness at the Crucifixion. The Descent of the Angel (xxviii. 2-4) adds richer and more imaginative colours to the story of the Resurrection, while the stories of the Guard (xxvii. 62-6, xxviii. 11-5) are designed to meet Jewish objections. These late stories are outgrowths from the Markan tradition; they mark the beginnings of Christian legend, although a gulf still divides them from the stories of the Apocryphal Gospels.

The result, then, of our inquiry is that there are signs

of three Passion Stories in the Gospels. Mark tells the Story as he had heard it in Palestine, and as it became current at Rome; John adapts the Story of Ephesus; Luke's Story is also that of a definite community, and the best suggestion is that it is the Passion Story of Caesarea.[1]

III

I pass now to the question of the relation between the Gospel records and the earliest oral Passion Stories. What changes have the Evangelists effected, and, in particular, have they inserted narratives and sayings which at one time circulated separately?

Let me say at once that anything we can advance in answer to this question is largely a matter of conjecture. I believe, however, that up to a point the conjectures are valid and useful. So far as the Fourth Gospel is concerned, there is little scope for investigation. The Evangelist's use of sources is so free that it will never be possible to penetrate far beyond the Fourth Gospel itself. In the case of the Third Gospel the project is more hopeful. The first step is that of setting aside all that has been added from Mark.[2] We cannot assume, however, that by this simple process we reach the Passion

[1] Cf. *B.T.G.* 211-4, and see Acts xxi. 8-10, 15, 17; xxiii. 23, 33; xxiv. 27; xxvii. 1 f.

[2] Most of the fourteen passages I have described as 'Markan insertions' are also treated as such by B. H. Streeter and B. S. Easton; but, in addition, these scholars essay the more difficult task of indicating Lukan passages which have been partly assimilated to the Markan text. In such matters it is not surprising that investigators differ; for even totally independent versions of the same incident would share common words, and it is not always easy to say when the limits of natural coincidence are exceeded.

Story as Luke found it; we have still to allow for the stylistic and material changes which he made in his source. The purely stylistic changes are not of serious moment, and for the most part can easily be detected. The possibility that Luke added sections to the Caesarean Story is more interesting and important. It arises in the case of stories which are loosely related to their context. The story of the Weeping Women (xxiii. 27-31), for example, has the form of a Pronouncement-Story, and the account of the Penitent Thief (xxiii. 39-43) is a story about Jesus which could be told apart from the Passion Narrative as a whole. It is reasonable, therefore, to think that these stories, and perhaps that of Herod and Jesus (xxiii. 6-16), are Lukan additions. Further, the short discourse sections which follow the account of the Supper (xxii. 24-38) look very much like excerpts from a collection of sayings; and there is force in the suggestion that in the Caesarean Story the words about eating and drinking in the Messianic Kingdom (vv. 28-30) immediately followed the declaration of Jesus that He would no more drink of the fruit of the vine until the Kingdom of God should come (v. 18). Beyond suggestions such as these it is hardly possible to go. In considering whether Luke is likely to have introduced material changes into his source, our views are naturally determined by our estimate of his literary methods in general. Luke's methods vary. Where he has good sources at his command he follows them with great fidelity[1]; but where his information is limited,

---

[1] So most British scholars. This opinion has also recently been confirmed by the researches of Bussmann, *S.Sn.* iii. 179.

and the interest is tense, he dramatises the story.[1] These principles are not contradictory, and both have to be taken into account in judging the Lukan Passion Story. The dramatic element is present in the story of the Agony[2] and in the Crucifixion scene; in other respects, notably in the accounts of the Arrest, the Mocking, and the Trial before the Priests, Luke appears to have had information which is superior to that of Mark, and the presumption is that he is following his source closely. On the question as a whole, we may justly conclude that Luke's artistic gifts have embellished, but have not distorted, the Caesarean Story.

In the Markan Story we face a question to which more attention has been directed. Even Dibelius (*F.E.* 57) recognizes that the story of the Anointing (xiv. 3-9) stands apart from the cycle in which it appears; and K. L. Schmidt (*R.G.J.* 307f.), no less strong an upholder of the continuity of the Markan Passion Story, sees additions in the Anointing, the Priests' Plot (xiv. 1f.), the Treachery of Judas (xiv. 10f.), and the phrase 'one of the twelve' in xiv. 43 (cf. xiv. 10). Bultmann goes much further (*G.S.T.* 282-308). It is impossible in this lecture to describe in detail his analysis of the Markan Story. In substance, it amounts to the recognition of an original kernel of connected material which told

---

[1] 'Whenever (Luke) describes an important spiritual event which he did not personally witness, he adopts a dramatic method of narration', F. J. Foakes-Jackson, *The Moffatt N. T. Commentary; the Acts*, 1931, p. 4.

[2] Streeter's argument (*F.G.* 137ff.) for the genuineness of xxii. 43f. is very forcible. If the passage is an interpolation, it is worth considering if it is not an element from Caesarean tradition which has found its way into the Lukan text.

quite briefly of the Arrest, the Condemnation by the
Sanhedrim and by Pilate, the Journey to the Cross, the
Crucifixion and Death. Later this account was supplemented by the addition of the Denial and the Prophecy
of the Denial (xiv. 27-31). It was also united with a
complex of stories which grouped themselves round the
Supper, and which then received a new introduction in
xiv. 1f., 10f. Still later were added the stories of the
Anointing (xiv. 3-9), Gethsemane (xiv. 32-42), and
probably the Trial before the Priests (xiv. 55-64), but
when the Crucifixion scene was expanded and rounded
off by the stories of the Women (xv. 40f.) and the
Burial (xv. 42-7) cannot be decided.

It is fair to say that the confidence with which Bultmann tells how the Markan Story came into being could
be justified only by the gift of omniscience. None the
less, the broad suggestion of a short original account
which was gradually enlarged, is reasonable in itself and
is supported by the literary phenomena. It is quite
likely that religious and apologetic interests have left
their mark on the record; but I do not believe that the
process is one of growth by legendary accretion. If
this were so, we should find contrasts in the material
comparable to those which appear in the Matthaean
Story, in stories like the Earthquake and the Resurrection of the Saints; and such elements are not present, except in the statement which may, however, have been
originally a Pauline comment: 'And the veil of the
temple was rent in twain from the top to the bottom'
(xv. 38). The facts would appear to be that the primitive sketch of the Arrest, Condemnation, Crucifixion,

and Death, awakened latent memories of other incidents which by degrees found their place within the communal Story. In other words, the historical nucleus attracted to itself traditional elements in free circulation, and brought them within the range of its own orbit.

IV

I pass now to the question why the Resurrection-tradition consisted of isolated stories, when the Passion Stories were early and continuous in form. Here I should like to make a suggestion which I think is new, but which is justified in the light of conclusions already reached. I have argued that the necessities of early preaching and of worship demanded a continuous Passion Story, that there could be little profit in telling a single story like the Arrest or the Mocking, since the centre of interest was the Crucified Lord, and how He came to His Cross. It is important to recall this, because we see at once that in the case of the Resurrection the position was quite different. Here the immediate need was assurance about a new and astounding fact. Was it true that Jesus had risen and had appeared to His own? To satisfy this clamant need single stories were enough; there was no demand for a continuous Story such as the modern man desires. Testimony, witness-bearing to the fact of the Appearances, was the first essential for preachers and hearers alike. We can understand therefore that different cycles of stories would become current at various centres of Palestinian and Syrian Christianity, but that there would be no continuous account which traced the succession of events from the Tomb to the final parting of Jesus from His disciples.   Naturally, there would be a preference for local stories, or for those associated with persons known to the community in question.   Thus, from the beginning, the way was prepared for the inevitable cleavage between the Jerusalem and Galilean traditions which is a subject for endless discussion among historians and exegetes.   The earliest tradition was not a record, but consisted of lists of Appearances and single stories.   We can see this from the list which Paul supplies in I Cor. xv. 4-8, and the accounts of his own experience in Acts xxii. and xxvi.   The same conclusion is required from the accounts in the Gospels.   These differ and defy our attempts at reconciliation and co-ordination, and they do this because the Evangelists were dependent on local tradition as it existed; they wanted to give a continuous story, but they could not do this, because the time for it was past; the materials for its accomplishment no longer existed.

These inferences are confirmed by a study of Lk. xxiv. In this chapter the Appearances are all associated with Jerusalem and its environs; there are no Galilean stories. Moreover, the connecting-links are editorial.   Verse 13 begins well with the statement that 'two of them were going that very day to a village named Emmaus', but in verse 34 an Appearance to Simon is mentioned of which until now we have heard nothing.   In the next story the eleven and the rest are 'terrified and affrighted' when Jesus appears in the midst of them, and suppose that they behold 'a spirit' (verse 37); and the immediate sequel to the incident is the parting of Jesus from His disciples over against Bethany (verses 50-3). We are driven to suppose that the Evangelist means to bring all the events narrated within a space of twenty-four hours, a view which he afterwards modifies in the reference to 'forty days' in Acts i. 3.

These facts are no longer mysterious when they are seen in the light of the considerations I have urged. When Luke penned this chapter, he had at his disposal the fragmentary tradition of a local Church. From the stories that were current he selected four, the Empty Tomb, the Journey to Emmaus, the Appearance to the Eleven, the Parting of Jesus. He took these stories as he found them, though, judging from the Emmaus story, we must suppose that he did not leave them as he found them. Probably, the original form was too rough; there were gaps, incoherences, contradictions, disconcerting silences; but shining through all was the conviction that Jesus had been loosed from the pangs of death 'because it was not possible that he should be holden of it'. Luke takes this material, arranges, expands, and embellishes it, to form the conclusion of his narrative. He describes the joyful tidings of the women, the amazing discovery of the disconsolate travellers, the assurance brought to the affrighted eleven and the charge to become witnesses to 'all the nations' when 'clothed with power from on high'. Finally, he tells of the Parting and leaves us with the picture of the disciples 'continually in the temple, blessing God'. Have we not in all this a glimpse, not only of the Evangelist at work, but of the conditions of the primitive period in a typical community? All is determined by the needs, practical, religious, and apologetic of the first Christians, and the tradition is continuous or fragmentary as the needs dictate.

The historical issues of these studies are both interesting and important. We learn to relate what we find in the Gospels to the life of the primitive period. We see that, while they are late, the Gospels arise out of early oral tradition. Difficulties in the accounts become plainer to us, not because they are always solved, but because we see why they exist. By comparing the different Passion Stories, in Mark, Luke, and John, we can more hopefully discuss points connected with the Supper, the Trial, the Crucifixion, and the Resurrection. Most important of all, we appreciate the place which the Story of the Passion held in the mind and affections of primitive Christianity, and so bring the account of Gospel Origins into closer contact with the situation as it is implied in the Pauline Epistles. If, finally, problems relating to the Empty Tomb, and the Resurrection Body of Jesus, remain as perplexing as ever, we see that the first Christians grasped what is as fundamental for us as it was for them—the assurance that Jesus conquered death, and 'shewed himself alive after his passion by many proofs' (Acts i. 3).

IV

PRONOUNCEMENT-STORIES

Iɴ this lecture I propose to examine the short narratives I have called 'Pronouncement-Stories'. Their chief characteristic, it will be remembered, is that they culminate in a saying of Jesus which expresses some ethical or religious precept; the saying may be evoked by a question friendly or otherwise, or may be associated with an incident which is indicated in very few words. Prized because they gave guidance to the first Christians, these stories circulated as single units of tradition, or were combined in groups on a purely topical thread.

Our first duty is to examine the material with which we have to deal, and since Bultmann has discussed it much more fully than either Dibelius or Albertz, it will be best to examine the two groups of his *Apophthegmata*.

I

Bultmann's first group[1] consists of twenty-four stories, sixteen of which appear also in the lists of Dibelius or Albertz. Of the sixteen stories, one, the Dropsical Man, is recorded by Luke alone (xiv. 1-6), and a second, the Baptist's Question (Lk. vii. 19ff. = Mt. xi. 2ff.), comes from Q. The remaining fourteen stories are

[1] *Streitgespräche* and *Schulgespräche*. See Lect. ii. p. 24.

Markan: the Paralytic (ii. 3ff.), Eating with Publicans and Sinners (ii. 15ff.), Fasting (ii. 18ff.), Cornfields on the Sabbath Day (ii. 23ff.), the Man with the Withered Hand (iii. 1ff.), the Beelzebub Controversy (iii. 22ff.)[1], Clean and Unclean (vii. 5ff.), Divorce (x. 2ff.), the Rich Man (x. 17 ff.), the Sons of Zebedee (x. 35 ff.), Authority (xi. 27ff.), Tribute-money (xii. 13ff.), the Resurrection (xii. 18ff.) and the Great Commandment (xii. 28ff.)[2]. All these stories reward study, but it is not possible now to examine more than one or two.

The Tribute-money (Mk. xii. 13ff.) illustrates the Pronouncement-Story at its best.

'And they send unto him certain of the Pharisees and of the Herodians, that they might catch him in talk. And when they were come, they say unto him, "Master, we know that thou art true, and carest not for any one: for thou regardest not the person of men, but of a truth teachest the way of God: Is it lawful to give tribute unto Caesar, or not? Shall we give, or shall we not give?" But he, knowing their hypocrisy, said unto them, "Why tempt ye me? bring me a penny, that I may see it". And they brought it. And he saith unto them, "Whose is this image and superscription?" And they said unto him, "Caesar's". And Jesus said unto them, "Render unto Caesar the things that are Caesar's, and unto God the things that are God's". And they marvelled greatly at him.'

This section, which is longer than many Pronouncement-Stories, is a perfect unity. It is the one story in this group where Bultmann sees no reason to think of a community-formation (*G.S.T.* 25). There is not the slightest interest in individuals, or in questions of time

---

[1]Also in Q (Lk. xi. 14ff. = Mt. xii. 22ff.).   [2]Also in Q (Lk. x. 25ff.).

or place.   Everything leads up to the final word of
Jesus, which for the early Christians must have had the
force of a pronouncement.   So Jesus had spoken, and
there was no more to be said!

Precisely the same features appear in Mk. xi. 27-33
(Authority), Mk. xii. 18-27 (the Resurrection), and
Mk. xii. 28-34 (the Great Commandment), except that
Mark, or an earlier compiler, has added a few com-
ments for the benefit of the reader (in xi. 27, xii. 18, 28,
34).

Most of the stories are of this type, but sometimes, as
in that of the Man with the Withered Hand (Mk. iii.
1-5), the pronouncement is expressed in the action of
Jesus more than in His words.

'He saith unto the man, "Stretch forth thy hand".   And he
stretched it forth: and his hand was restored.'

This narrative is distinguished from a Miracle-Story
by the fact that the healing is not related for itself, but
almost incidentally and for its bearing on the principal
point of interest, the question of the observance of the
Sabbath.

How secondary the narrative-interest can be, is well
illustrated in stories where a reference to the questioners
is the sole descriptive element (cf. the Beelzebub Controversy, Mk. iii. 22-6; Clean and Unclean, Mk. vii.
5-8; Divorce, Mk. x. 2-9), and where more detail is
given, it merely supplies the necessary background for
the question and answer (cf. Eating with Publicans,
Mk. ii. 15-7; Fasting, Mk. ii. 18-20; Cornfields, Mk.
ii. 23-6; the Dropsical Man, Lk. xiv. 1-6).   Where the

E

amount of detail is greater still, the question whether the original oral form was not shorter inevitably arises, as, for example, in the Baptist's Question (cf. Lk. vii. 20f.).   The problem is still more apparent in the Sons of Zebedee (Mk. x. 35-40) to which, presumably, Mark has attached other sayings (cf. vv. 41-5), and where Matthew (xx. 20) has introduced the mother of James and John.   When we compare the Synoptic forms of the Rich Man, we see a Pronouncement-Story on wealth which is already coming to be a Story about Jesus.   The man who in Mk. x. 17 runs and kneels, is described in Mt. xix. 22 as a 'young man', and in Lk. xviii. 18 as 'a certain ruler', while in the Apocryphal *Gospel according to the Hebrews* he is one of two questioners, and at the demand of Jesus to sell all he begins 'to scratch his head' in his displeasure and perplexity (*A.N.T.* 6).

The story of the Healing of the Paralytic (Mk. ii. 3-12) has peculiar features of its own.   It has often been pointed out that the words 'saith unto the sick of the palsy' in verse 5 are awkwardly repeated in verse 10, and it has frequently been suggested that the intervening verses are an interpolation.   Stated in this form the suggestion is absurd, for the intervening matter on the forgiveness of sins reads like good tradition, and is the main topic of the section.   None the less the peculiar construction is there, and the incident is related in much greater detail than is usual, or necessary, in a Pronouncement-Story.   Is the solution found in the suggestion that the story circulated in two forms, both as a Miracle-Story and a Pronouncement-Story?   It is significant that if we bring the sundered phrases together, and reduce them to one, we gain a perfect Miracle-Story.

'And they come, bringing unto him a man sick of the palsy, borne of four. And when they could not come nigh unto him for the crowd, they uncovered the roof where he was: and when they had broken it up, they let down the bed whereon the sick of the palsy lay. And Jesus seeing their faith saith unto the sick of the palsy, "I say unto thee, Arise, take up thy bed, and go unto thy house". And he arose, and straightway took up the bed, and went forth before them all; insomuch that they were all amazed, and glorified God, saying, "We never saw it on this fashion".'

This narrative has all the marks of the Miracle-Story —an introduction describing the sufferer and the circumstances, the account of the cure, and a brief description of the result, including a confirmation of the cure and a reference to the effect produced on the onlookers. If we now look at the intervening matter we see that it is a Pronouncement-Story from which the beginning and the end are missing.

'. . . And (Jesus) saith unto the sick of the palsy, "Son, thy sins are forgiven". But there were certain of the scribes sitting there, and reasoning in their hearts, "Why doth this man thus speak? he blasphemeth: who can forgive sins but one, even God?" And straightway Jesus, perceiving in his spirit that they so reasoned within themselves, saith unto them, "Why reason ye these things in your hearts? Whether is easier, to say to the sick of the palsy, Thy sins are forgiven; or to say, Arise, and take up thy bed, and walk? But that ye may know that the Son of man hath power on earth to forgive sins . . .".'

That is as far as we can trace the story, but I submit that the sequel must have been a cure, but related more briefly than in the existing story.   For here, as distinct from a Miracle-Story, the main interest is not the cure, but the question of the forgiveness of sins, which is raised by an inquiry visible in the faces of the scribes and answered by Jesus in word and deed.   I suggest that before Mark wrote his Gospel, the original beginning and end of the Pronouncement-Story were cut away and replaced by the fuller details of the Miracle-Story.   And this hypothesis is the less bold, as we shall see later that the whole section Mk. ii. 1–iii. 6 is, as Albertz maintains, a pre-Markan collection of *Streitgespräche* designed to show how inevitable the tragic fate of Jesus was.

There are other interesting points connected with these sixteen stories, but enough has been said to show that, apart from literary adjustments, they are all true Pronouncement-Stories which concern points of moral and religious importance for the first Christians.   I will therefore turn to the eight stories which are peculiar to Bultmann's first group.   These are the Strange Exorcist, the Withered Fig Tree, the Bent Woman, the Woman in the City, the Question about the Inheritance, the Murder of the Galileans, the Coming of the Kingdom, and the Samaritan Village.   The first two are Markan; the rest are peculiar to Luke.

The Strange Exorcist (Mk. ix. 38f.) is surely a Pronouncement-Story, for John's statement is immediately followed by the reply of Jesus, 'Forbid him not . . .', and there can be little doubt that it is for the sake of this word of Jesus that the story was told: its value for the first Christians needs no argument.   The story of the

Withered Fig Tree (Mk. xi. 20-5) makes a much less favourable impression, because some of the sayings in 22ff. on faith and prayer are found in Matthew and Luke in other contexts, and appear to be isolated sayings which have been loosely strung together and appended to the present story. Here, I think, Bultmann is right when he suggests that the basis of the whole is a Miracle-Story, the original significance of which is obscure; and for this reason I do not propose to include Mk. xi. 20-5 among the Pronouncement-Stories. Four of the Lukan stories raise little difficulty. The story of the Bent Woman is not told for its own sake but on account of the words of Jesus about the Sabbath (Lk. xiii. 15f.); in the Question about the Inheritance (Lk. xii. 13f.) and the Murder of the Galileans (Lk. xiii. 1-5), the narrative element is merely sufficient to introduce the words of Jesus; while the Coming of the Kingdom (Lk. xvii. 20f.) is prefaced in the barest possible manner by the words: 'And being asked (by the Pharisees), when the kingdom of God cometh, he answered them and said'. The remaining two Lukan stories raise difficult problems, but in different ways. In the story of the Samaritan Village (Lk. ix. 52b-6) textual problems confuse the issue. In its commonly accepted form the story ends with the words: 'But he turned and rebuked them. And they went to another village'; but between these sentences important MSS. give the sayings: 'Ye know not what manner of spirit ye are of', and 'For the Son of man came not to destroy men's lives, but to save them'. If these words belong to the text, or to any earlier form of it, the story is a Pronouncement-Story, and the tenor of

the sayings, and the fact that both appear in the Caesarean text (Θ) and the first also in the Western text (D),
support this view. The difficulty of ascribing the
words to Luke is that important Alexandrian MSS.
(אBC) omit them, while the suggestion of Zahn that they
were omitted by an anti-Marcionite scribe is not very
convincing. Perhaps the best view to take is that
which sees glimpses of an earlier Pronouncement-Story
which by the time Luke wrote his Gospel had become a
narrative proper. In this case the emergence of the
sayings in D and Θ is the return of an older traditional
form.

The story of the Woman in the City (Lk. vii. 36-50)
also presents difficulties. As it stands the narrative is
much too complex to be regarded as a Pronouncement-
Story. We are, however, appreciably nearer a popular
form in 36-40 + 44-7*a*; and this fact adds force to the
frequently made suggestion that the Parable of the Two
Debtors, and all that goes with it (47*b*, 'but to whom
little is forgiven . . .'), are editorial additions. This
view is certainly better than Bultmann's suggestion that
in the story pictorial clothing is given to the parable on
the basis of Mk. xiv. 3-9 (the Anointing). In this case
a different story ought to have been composed, since the
teaching of the parable is that love is the *result* of forgiveness whereas in the existing story love is the *ground*
of forgiveness (47*a*, 'for she loved much'). The simplest explanation is that two similar, but really discor-
dant, pieces of tradition have been combined in Luke's
special source. This, as we have seen, is not the only
case where a Pronouncement-Story appears to be one of

the constituent elements in a complex narrative.   I suggest then that neither the Woman in the City nor the Samaritan Village is a Pronouncement-Story as it stands, but that each seems to have been preceded by such a story in the oral period.

II

I turn now to the twenty biographical *Apophthegmata* of Bultmann's second group.   These stories raise greater problems; the narrative element is considerably larger, and it is often difficult to decide whether a particular section is a Pronouncement-Story or a Story about Jesus.   Fascher (*F.M.* 203) suggests that we should classify them under the sub-title *Anekdoten*, but the name, at least in its English form, is too ill-defined, and fails to do justice to the special character of these stories. Provided a narrative ends in a pronouncement of Jesus, expressed or implied, it does not matter materially whether it is introduced by a question or a description of events.   Indeed, in the narratives of the first group there are several in which there is a descriptive element, notably in those which refer to a healing.   In the stories now under review the point to decide is whether the narrative element is introduced for its own sake, or whether it is subordinate to a pronouncement, stated or implied.

Nine stories in this group appear to be true Pronouncement-Stories: the narrative element is not much more than a frame for the saying of Jesus.   This is so in the story of the Kindred of Jesus (Mk. iii. 31-5).

'And there come his mother and his brethren; and, standing without, they sent unto him, calling him.   And a multitude was sitting about him; and they say unto him, "Behold, thy mother and thy brethren without seek for thee".   And he answereth them, and saith, "Who is my mother and my brethren?"   And looking round on them which sat round about him, he saith, "Behold, my mother and my brethren!   For whosoever shall do the will of God, the same is my brother, and sister, and mother".'

A little more detail is added in vv. 19*b*-21, if these words belong to the story, for here we learn that the kindred of Jesus thought that He was 'beside himself' and in need of restraint; but the whole is told, not for the sake of giving information, but to prepare the way for the saying of Jesus.

The story of the Blessing of the Mother of Jesus (Lk. xi. 27f.) is very similar.

'And it came to pass, (as he said these things), a certain woman out of the multitude lifted up her voice, and said unto him, "Blessed is the womb that bare thee, and the breasts which thou didst suck".   But he said, "Yea rather, blessed are they that hear the word of God, and keep it".'

It is often said that these stories are tradition-variants. If this is so it suggests that the narrative element is determined by a selective process; and it is to be expected, rather than otherwise, that in two versions of the same story different details taken from the original facts will lead up to what is substantially the same saying.

Equally with these stories, those of the Candidates for Discipleship (Lk. ix. 57-62 = Mt. viii. 19-22), the Blessing of the Children (Mk. x. 13-6), and the Widow's Mites (Mk. xii. 41-4) are Pronouncement-Stories.   So to describe the Candidates for Discipleship is at once to understand the peculiarities of this story; we see why the men are so vaguely described.   The first Christians were not interested in these men, but in the words of Jesus.   For them these words had a present significance, for they knew that following Jesus sometimes meant the loss of a settled home and the breaking of family ties.   The Blessing of the Children was told because the words of Jesus defined the place of children in the Kingdom, and the Widow's Mites because it expressed His mind on the subject of almsgiving.

I next invite your attention to two stories which bear on the relations of the first Christians with Judaism. The first of these is the Prophecy of the Destruction of the Temple (Mk. xiii. 1f.).

'And as he went forth out of the temple, one of his disciples saith unto him, "Master, behold, what manner of stones and what manner of buildings!"   And Jesus said unto him, "Seest thou these great buildings? there shall not be left here one stone upon another, which shall not be thrown down".'

There is no real justification for regarding this story as 'a prophecy after the event', for that Jesus foretold the destruction of the city is deeply inwrought in the tradition and is adequately explained as a mark of His insight.   Interest in the story would hardly be characteristic of the period when Christians still joined in the Temple worship (Acts ii. 46; iii. 1), but the situation must have been changed as the breach between the Synagogue and the Church widened.   The other story is that of the Temple-tax (Mt. xvii. 24-7).   It is usual to class this story with the *narratives* peculiar to Matthew, but I very much doubt if this classification is right.   The narrative is rather a Pronouncement-

Story[1]; it defines the attitude Christians are to take to the Temple dues. Kings' sons are free, but in order not to give offence the half-shekel should be paid from the fruits of toil. A story like this must have proved useful in difficult days when the relation of Christianity to Judaism was a burning question. It is astonishing that the narrative was never turned into a Miracle-Story. Had it belonged to the narrative tradition peculiar to Matthew, I doubt if it could have escaped this fate, and for this reason I now prefer to think that it belonged to the M source; its character as a Pronouncement-Story shielded it against legendary amplifications.

A Pronouncement-Story of another character is the narrative of the Anointing (Mk. xiv. 3-9). Here an incident gives rise to a question to which Jesus replies in words treasured by the first Christians:

'Let her alone; why trouble ye her? she hath wrought a good work on me. For ye have the poor always with you, and whensoever ye will ye can do them good: but me ye have not always. She hath done what she could: she hath anointed my body aforehand for the burying.'

Whether the original story contained the words about the burial is often questioned. To me the words look more like a characteristic word of Jesus than the inspired addition of a redactor; the redactor's hand is more probably present in the command for the repetition of the story (v. 9). It should be observed how well the

---

[1]It is unusual in Pronouncement-Stories to find personal and place names, and the references to Peter and Capernaum may be later elements. But these points may be present because the story belonged to a Petrine cycle of tradition.

recognition of the section as a Pronouncement-Story agrees with the view that it existed apart from the earliest Passion Story as a self-contained unit of tradition.[1] The same is true of the story of the Weeping Women of Jerusalem in the Lukan Passion Story (xxiii. 27-31). This, too, is a Pronouncement-Story. No question is put to Jesus, but His words arise out of the situation, and their eschatological cast suggests that the story was told in a primitive community which looked forward to the Parousia.

The only other story in this group which might be classified as a Pronouncement-Story is the narrative of the Ten Lepers (Lk. xvii. 11-9). This reaches its climax in the words:

'Were there none found that returned to give glory to God, save this stranger?';

but the words may be the application of a Miracle-Story, and, in any case, its relation to the Markan story of the Leper (i. 40-5) must always remain obscure.

The remaining ten stories in Bultmann's second list seem to me to be Stories about Jesus rather than Pronouncement-Stories. One of them, the story of the Centurion's Servant (Lk. vii. 2-10 = Mt. viii. 5-13), is from Q. Four are from Mark: the Calling of the First Disciples (i. 16-20; ii. 14), the Rejection at Nazareth (vi. 1-6), the Syro-Phoenician Woman (vii. 24-30), and the Cleansing (xi. 15-7); and the remaining five are found in Luke alone: Martha and Mary (x. 38-42), Jesus and Herod (xiii. 31-3), Zacchaeus (xix. 1-10), the Rejoicing

[1]See p. 57.

of the Disciples (xix. 39f.), and the Weeping over Jerusalem (xix. 41-4). In these stories the interest appears
to lie in the incidents themselves rather than in the words
of Jesus. Again, more detail than is usual in Pronouncement-Stories is supplied, and where this is not
the case, as in the two Lukan stories of the Rejoicing of
the Disciples and the Weeping over Jerusalem, the sections appear to be literary compositions rather than popular stories. Further, except in the case of the Calling
of the First Disciples, the stories are less directly related
to the practical and religious interests in the life-situation of the first Christians. The two stories about
which one will hesitate most are those of the Centurion's
Servant and the Syro-Phoenician Woman, since in both
stories the faith manifested by Gentiles, rather than
the miracles of healing, appears to be the main point
of interest.[1] Neither is a Pronouncement-Story as it
stands, but once more the question is raised whether
they had this form at one time in the oral period. In
this respect the two stories resemble those of the Samaritan Village and the Woman in the City.

I have now mentioned all Bultmann's examples, and I
think it will be agreed that, while difficult questions
arise in the case of individual stories, the problems are
fewer than might have been expected. With some confidence I would claim that his two groups contain at

[1]In discussing the Centurion's Servant, Harnack suggested that Q
either did not mention the cure or described it in terms other than those
of Lk. vii. 10 or Mt. viii. 13*b*. Cf. *The Sayings of Jesus*, p. 210. In
its Lukan form the story has received additions (cf. vii. 3-5); in Matthew
the saying about many from the east and the west has been added from
another part of Q (cf. Mt. viii. 11f. = Lk. xiii. 28f.).

least thirty Pronouncement-Stories, and traces of four
others.   We must now inquire if more stories of the
kind are indicated by Dibelius and Albertz.

III

Only two of the *Paradigmen* of Dibelius fail to appear
in Bultmann's lists.   The first, the story of the Demoniac in the Synagogue at Capernaum (Mk. i. 23ff.),
is really a Miracle-Story, and need not detain us.   The
second is the story of the Man working on the Sabbath,
which is found in Codex Bezae after Lk. vi. 4.

'(On the same day) he saw a man working on the Sabbath and
said unto him, "Man, if thou knowest what thou art doing,
blessed art thou; but if thou dost not know, thou art accursed and
a transgressor of the law".'

It has often been justly argued that this is a genuine
piece of oral tradition, which, because of its local currency or the boldness of its contents, did not find a place
in the Gospels.   To these arguments we may now add
the contention that it has the form of a Pronouncement-
Story, and treats the same question of the Sabbath
which several of these stories raise.

Albertz adds three stories: the Temptation, the
Davidic Sonship, and the Demand for a Sign.   He
rightly regards the Temptation (Lk. iv. 1-13 = Mt. iv.
1-11) as a *Streitgespräch*, for it is a polemical debate between Jesus and Satan; but as such it stands apart from
everything else in the Gospels,[1] and, I suggest, is best

[1] The sayings it contains are mainly significant for an understanding of
the Mission and Person of Jesus rather than as principles determining
daily conduct or illustrating questions of faith.

classified as a Story about Jesus rather than as a Pronouncement-Story.

The structure of the story about the Davidic Sonship (Mk. xii. 35-7) is unusual, in that both the question and the answer are supplied by Jesus.[1]

'And Jesus answered and said, (as he taught in the temple), "How say the scribes that the Christ is the son of David?   David himself said in the Holy Spirit,

'The Lord said unto my Lord,
Sit thou on my right hand,
Till I make thine enemies the footstool of thy feet.'

David himself calleth him Lord; and whence is he his son?".'

This variation in form is due, either to the facts of the story, or to the editorial work of Mark, who has already recorded four stories in which there is an interplay of question and answer between Jesus and His opponents. In any case the story is a Pronouncement-Story; it shows what Jesus thought of the relationship between Messiahship and mere physical descent from David; and, in the period before the Genealogies were compiled, it may well have been used by Christians in controversy with Jews who laid stress on the necessity of actual physical descent.

The story of the Demand for a Sign (Mk. viii. 11f.) opens with the statement that the Pharisees came forth and began to question with him 'seeking of him a

[1]It is interesting to observe that Matthew (xxii. 41-5) turns the story into the more usual form.   Jesus asks: 'What think ye of the Christ? whose son is he?'   The Pharisees reply 'The Son of David', and the story proceeds as in Mark.   This fact is a reminder that other things than structure have to be taken into account in discussing Pronouncement-Stories.

sign from heaven, tempting him'; and it ends with the words:

'And he sighed deeply in his spirit, and saith, "Why doth this generation seek a sign? verily I say unto you, There shall no sign be given unto this generation".'

This story must have been current because it rebuked those who sighed for signs and wonders. Like the last example, it may also have been used in controversy with Jews, for besides the healing-stories and the nature-miracles of Mark, the first Christians had nothing to offer to any one who demanded a portent by which Jesus authenticated His claims in the course of His Ministry. For these reasons I suggest that the story is a Pronouncement-Story, but with the reservations demanded by our want of knowledge concerning the earliest times.

If these criticisms are just, we see that conjointly Dibelius and Albertz add three Pronouncement-Stories to those contained in the lists of Bultmann, two in Mark and one from the extra-Canonical tradition. We must next ask if any others, or traces of others, can be found in the Synoptic Gospels, and whether any appear in the Fourth Gospel.

IV

The three Form-Critics have covered the ground so fully that little material is left for further discussion. I would urge, however, that serious consideration ought to be given to the section on the Purpose of Parables in Mk. iv. 10-2.

'And when he was alone, they that were about him with the twelve asked of him the parables. And he said unto them,

"Unto you is given the mystery of the kingdom of God: but unto them that are without, all things are done in parables: that

> 'Seeing they may see, and not perceive;
> And hearing they may hear, and not understand;
> Lest haply they should turn again,
> And it should be forgiven them' "'.

It is not surprising that the Form-Critics do not offer this story as a 'paradigm' or an 'apophthegm'. Since Wrede[1] it has been common to explain this passage as a dogmatic addition of Mark in the interests of his view that the Messiahship of Jesus was kept secret during the Ministry. So dominant is this theory in Germany that a critic who defends the passage takes his reputation into his hands. Both Dibelius[2] and Bultmann[3] are deeply influenced by Wrede's theory; but in this they do violence, as Form-Critics, to their own principles. For the section has the form of a Pronouncement-Story, and can be related to the life-situation of the first Christians.[4] By no means all the parables are easy of interpretation, and we cannot suppose that the first Christians found them so. If, then, such a story as Mk. iv. 10-2 existed, it could be used by those who wanted to account for the obscurity of parables. No reason, moreover, can be given why Jesus should not have used the words of Isa. vi. 10. No more than Isaiah himself will He have meant to speak of concealment as His purpose; but He may well have ironically spoken of what in some cases

[1] *Das Messiasgeheimnis in den Evangelien*, 1901.

[2] Dibelius, *F.E.* 62, 64.   [3] Bultmann, *G.S.T.* 215, 351.

[4] It is not consistent to describe Mark as a mere collector, as Dibelius does (*F.E.* 2), and then to credit him with creative dogmatic tendencies (*F.E.* 62ff.).

was the actual result of teaching by parables in the classical words of Isaiah.[1]

A question of another kind arises in the case of some of the isolated sayings: may they not be the remains of Pronouncement-Stories from which all narrative matter has fallen away? The words attached to the Cornfields story will serve as an illustration (Mk. ii. 27f.):

'And he said unto them, "The sabbath was made for man, and not man for the sabbath: so that the Son of man is lord even of the sabbath".'

It may be that the saying was current as an isolated word of Jesus, and was simply appended to the Cornfields story; but it is also possible that it formed the climax of a lost Pronouncement-Story. Naturally, in any given case this possibility cannot be tested; but the more often such questions arise, the more difficult they are to suppress. It is in every way credible that sayings became isolated in this manner; they are winged words detached from their context by the winds of time and circumstance. The thirty or forty Pronouncement-Stories in the Gospels can be only a fraction of those which existed in the oral period. Many must have perished through the weakness of human memory; but the saying, the most virile element in the oral unit, would often survive, separated from the question which prompted it and the account of the events out of which it sprang. This explanation may be the key to the complex of sayings in Mk. vii. 1-23. The opening statements (vv. 1-4) are probably the work of the Evangelist;

[1]For an alternative explanation of Mk. iv. 10ff. see T. W. Manson, *T.J.* 75-80.

F

but the next section is a Pronouncement-Story on the subject of the tradition of the Elders (vv. 5-8). The point of immediate interest lies in the four short sections which follow this story (9-13, 14-5, 17-9, 20-3), all of which consist mainly of sayings dealing with some aspect of the same theme. May not these sections be fragments of Pronouncement-Stories, cut down by the compiler, or reduced to their present form by the action of time?

In the Fourth Gospel there are no Pronouncement-Stories comparable to those in the Synoptics; and this is not surprising, in view of the late date of that Gospel and its literary interests. The nearest parallels are the controversial debates with the Jews at Jerusalem, of which Jn. x. 22-30 is a good example:

'And it was the feast of the dedication at Jerusalem: it was winter; and Jesus was walking in the temple in Solomon's porch. The Jews therefore came round about him, and said unto him, "How long dost thou hold us in suspense? If thou art the Christ, tell us plainly". Jesus answered them, "I told you, and ye believe not: the works that I do in my Father's name, these bear witness of me. But ye believe not, because ye are not of my sheep. My sheep hear my voice, and I know them, and they follow me: and I give unto them eternal life; and they shall never perish, and no one shall snatch them out of my hand. My Father, which hath given them unto me, is greater than all; and no one is able to snatch them out of my Father's hand. I and the Father are one".'

In this section a question is put and Jesus replies, but the answer has neither the brevity nor the relevancy of the Synoptic stories. New ideas are introduced which do not arise out of the situation, but remind us of other contexts; the section is not a self-contained unit, in spite of the fact that it reaches a climax in the words, 'I and the Father are one'. The subject-matter, moreover, is relevant rather to conditions at Ephesus at the close of the first century than to those of the first believers. In other words, while traditional materials may have been used, the section is a literary composition, not a spoken discourse.[1]

But, although the Fourth Gospel itself does not contain a Pronouncement-Story, by the accidents of textual transmission its text as commonly printed furnishes an example in the story of the Woman taken in Adultery (vii. 53–viii. 11).

'And the scribes and the Pharisees bring a woman taken in adultery; and having set her in the midst, they say unto him, "Master, this woman hath been taken in adultery, in the very act. Now in the law Moses commanded us to stone such: what then sayest thou of her?" And this they said, tempting him, that they might have whereof to accuse him. But Jesus stooped down, and with his finger wrote on the ground. But when they continued asking him, he lifted up himself, and said unto them, "He that is without sin among you, let him first cast a stone at her". And again he stooped down, and with his finger wrote on the ground. And they, when they heard it, went out one by one, beginning from the eldest, even unto the last: and Jesus was left alone, and the woman, where she was, in the midst. And Jesus lifted up himself, and said unto her, "Woman, where are they? did no man condemn thee?" And she said, "No man, Lord". And Jesus said, "Neither do I condemn thee: go thy way; from henceforth sin no more".'

[1]'Here is not the conflict of Jesus with the religion of His contemporaries, but the conflict of the Jews with the positions of the post-Apostolic, Hellenistic community', H. Windisch, *J.E.* 198.

This narrative is surely a Pronouncement-Story; the only question is whether all its details appeared in the oral story. Like the story of the Man working on the Sabbath, it is a unit of oral tradition which, because of its challenging character, or its limited currency, was not used by the Evangelists.[1] For us to-day the story is precious because it reveals the attitude of Jesus towards a sinful woman. So must it have been from the beginning. But among the first Christians it must have been valued because it disclosed His attitude to the Mosaic Law: Jesus does not annul the Law but reinterprets it just as He does in some of the great utterances of Mt. v. It is fitting that our investigation should close with this story. Its precarious place in the manuscript tradition reminds us of how much has perished. But enough remains to show us how great a place these stories filled in the life of primitive Christianity. As through a glass darkly we see men and women anxious to be guided by the word of the Lord who told and retold stories, not for details they contained but because they led swiftly to words of Jesus which for them were final, because they were His words and because they were words of life.

v

I shall leave to the final lecture questions relating to the collecting of Pronouncement-Stories into topical groups during the oral period. But before closing the present lecture I must discuss once more the historical

---

[1] D, alone among the early uncials, includes the story in the Fourth Gospel; 13 etc. place it after Lk. xxi. 38, and the vocabulary and style are Lukan rather than Johannine. Was it a unit of Caesarean tradition?

value of these stories. I have previously spoken of Bultmann's estimate, and have suggested that its negative character is due to over-concentration on matters of form and structure, and to an excessive reliance on the analogies presented by the Rabbinic tradition. Now that we have reviewed the stories ourselves we can see if this is not really the case. Bultmann thinks that many of the *Apophthegmata* have been spun out of sayings of Jesus by the imagination of the community, and that even where a story is a 'uniform conception' it is often 'ideal' in character. I cannot think that this opinion is supported by a study of the stories themselves. If it were a question whether an ideal element does not sometimes enter into the details of a narrative, as when, on occasion, nameless individuals are described as Scribes and Pharisees, it would be another and less important matter; a rejection which excludes all the stories, except a few like the Tribute-Money and the Anointing, is absurd. It is, as Fascher observes, really a question of what demands we make in respect of a historical report. 'If it must look like a legal formula or the registration of evidence which catalogues with exaggerated precision every trivial detail, there is no historical account in the entire New Testament, or indeed in most of our other historical sources. But if we are of the opinion that a report is historical which records that which is essential, we shall recognize many of them' (*F.M.* 105).

Bultmann's position is made all the more difficult by reason of his admissions. He claims that nearly all the *Apophthegmata* are Palestinian in origin, that purer forms are preserved in the Synoptic *Streitgespräche* than in the Rabbinic stories, and that the biographical *Apophthegmata* were 'paradigms' used in preaching to 'serve the living realisation of the Master' (*G.S.T.* 42, 49, 58, 63f.). Some of his objections are trivial, as when he asks how Jesus could observe what individuals gave at the Temple, or could know that the widow gave her all, how He was aware that the crowd murmured because He was the guest of Zacchaeus, and where and to whom He said, 'To-day is salvation come to this house, forasmuch as he also is a son of Abraham'. In such questions his own definition of *Apophthegmata* as 'pieces whose point is formed by a word of Jesus set in a short frame' is forgotten. The critic gives place to counsel for the prosecution.

The distribution of the Pronouncement-Stories has some bearing on the question of their early currency and genuineness. There are at least twenty in Mark, seven or nine in Luke's special source, four or five in Q,[1] one in Matthew, and none in John. If the stories are products of Christian imagination, why do they not increase in number as time passes, and as new problems confront the growing Church? Why is there no Pronouncement-Story about the necessity of the Cross, or the Gentile Mission, or the foundation and organization of the Church? The absence of these topics in the stories which have come down to us gives us reason to pause before views which credit the first Christians with a facility for invention and an imagination always at command. If Bultmann is right, Christian imagination was potent where it was least needed, feeble or wanting

[1]That is, in Q as Matthew and Luke found this source. See later pp. 182-4.

where silence called for its exercise; it left undone the
things which it ought to have done, and did the things it
had no need to do.

But the contents of the Pronouncement-Stories are
their sufficient guarantee.   Albertz is well justified in
claiming that the *Streitgespräche* are based on real inter-
views between Jesus and His contemporaries.   He
points out that the problems discussed are those of the
time—questions about Sabbath observance, divorce, the
tradition of the elders, fasting, tax-paying, the apocalyptic hope of the Resurrection, the One 'who should come'.
'It is', he says, 'the historical Jesus who is attacked, not
the Christ on whom the community believed' (*S.S.* 63).
Bultmann in no way shakes this contention when he says
that what Albertz gives with one hand when he speaks
of the original discourse, he takes back with the other
when he describes the characteristics of the existing narratives (*G.S.T.* 41); for the deficiencies of the narratives
are examples of the limitations which beset all historical
records, not proofs of the exercise of free imagination.
Far, then, from acquiescing in any denial of the historical element in these stories, we ought rather to esteem
them among the strongest and most stable elements in
the Gospel tradition.   They are not necessarily, on this
account, the most important elements in the tradition;
they are those which met immediate needs and were
most easily remembered; yet none the less they give a
singularly living portraiture of Jesus the Teacher and
the Prophet, and for us as for the first Christians preserve words final for guidance among thorny problems
of conduct and faith.

V

SAYINGS AND PARABLES

We have already seen what a large place the sayings filled in the earliest tradition, for even in
Mark at least twenty stories owe their existence
to the fact that they preserved sayings. This circumstance shows how wrong it is to think of Mark exclusively as a narrative Gospel in which a very secondary
interest is taken in the teaching of Jesus. This view is
plainly an exaggeration; Mark, as well as Matthew and
Luke, though in a different way, is a compend of the
things done and said by Jesus.

The sayings now to be considered are those which
have no narrative framework. I have suggested that
some of them represent all that now remains of lost Pronouncement-Stories, but, of course, this view does not
account for all the sayings. Jesus did not limit His
teaching to aphorisms and answers to questions; He
spoke in discourses and parables. From the beginning
then isolated sayings must have been current in Christian tradition. What Jesus said was remembered;
where it was said, and under what conditions, was less
easily recalled in circumstances less dramatic than those
associated with the Pronouncement-Stories.

I

1. Our first inquiry concerns the formal characteristics of individual sayings. In *The Poetry of our Lord* (1925) Canon Burney has shown how common parallelism, rhythm, and even rhyme are in the sayings of Mark, Q, and the Fourth Gospel. Synonymous parallelism, for example, is visible in such passages as Mt. v. 45 and Lk. xii. 22f. (= Mt. vi. 25):

> 'He maketh his sun to rise on the evil and the good,
> And sendeth rain on the just and the unjust.'

> 'Be not anxious for your life, what ye shall eat;
> Nor yet for your body, what ye shall put on.
> For the life is more than the food,
> And the body than the raiment.'

Antithetical parallelism is illustrated by Mt. vii. 17:

> 'Every good tree bringeth forth good fruit;
> But the corrupt tree bringeth forth evil fruit.'

Synthetic parallelism appears in couplets where the sense flows on continuously from the first line to the second, as in Mt. xxiii. 5:

> 'They make broad their phylacteries,
> And enlarge their fringes',

and Step-parallelism in Mt. x. 40:

> 'He that receiveth you, receiveth me;
> And he that receiveth me, receiveth him that sent me.'

These structural characteristics are so marked in the sayings of Jesus that Canon Burney feels justified in using them for the detection of glosses.   For example, in the saying 'Be not anxious for your life', Matthew adds the words 'or what ye shall drink', and so, says Canon Burney, 'destroys the balance of the couplet' (*P.L.* 67). He also claims that the forms have an important bearing on the question of genuineness.   Thus, of such a saying as Mt. x. 39:

> 'He that findeth his life shall lose it;
> And he that loseth his life for my sake shall find it',

he writes: 'In this and in similar forms of antithesis we may surely believe that we possess our Lord's *ipsissima verba* more nearly than in any sentence otherwise expressed'.   He also urges that the presence of Antithetic parallelism 'has an important bearing upon the authenticity of the discourses in the Fourth Gospel' (*P.L.* 84).   These inferences, I fear, go beyond the evidence because others, besides Jesus, might use these structural forms, as we see from the Prologue to the Fourth Gospel.   The true conclusion to draw is the important, but less ambitious claim that the form reveals the fundamentally Jewish character of the sayings. This result is also reached by P. Fiebig in a still more extensive study of forms.   'The Synoptic sayings', he declares, 'make a more living impression than the Rabbinical sayings'; 'Still more than the latter they bear in themselves the echo of living speech' (*E.E.* 31 *n.*).

2. From isolated couplets and quatrains I turn next to groups of sayings where the arrangement seems to be artificial.   Mk. iv. 21-5 appears to be a group of this character:

'(And he said unto them),
"Is the lamp brought to be put under the bushel, or
            under the bed,
And not to be put on the stand?

"For there is nothing hid, save that it should be mani-
            fested;
Neither was anything made secret, but that it should
            come to light.

"If any man hath ears to hear, let him hear".

(And he said unto them),
"Take heed what ye hear:

"With what measure ye mete,
It shall be measured unto you:
And more shall be given unto you.

"For he that hath, to him shall be given:
And he that hath not, from him shall be taken away
            even that which he hath".'

There is every reason to think that this section of
Mark is an excerpt from a collection of sayings. It appears abruptly in the chapter, separating the parables of
the Seed growing Secretly and the Mustard Seed from
that of the Sower; and the connexion with its present
context is remote. Further, the group itself appears to
be an artificial compilation: each saying has a genuine
ring, but the arrangement is determined by catchwords
and by similarities which lie on the surface. The sayings on the Lamp and on the Purpose of Hiding stand
side by side because they have to do with the ideas of
concealment and light; and the sayings, 'With what
measure ye mete' and 'He that hath', because they

embody the thought of gain and loss. Such an arrangement offers an irresistible lure to the skill of commentators who want to discover a subtle succession of thought; but the ingenuity is wasted and only repeats the work of the compiler. Not so did Jesus speak when the people heard Him gladly; the arrangement is that which we find repeatedly in Proverbs, Ecclesiastes, and the Wisdom of Sirach.

If we have any doubts about this view they are dispelled by a study of other groups of sayings in Mark, such as viii. 34–ix. 1 and ix. 41-50. In the second group especially the presence of catchwords like 'little ones', 'stumbling', 'fire', and 'salt' is unmistakable. Every link is genuine, but the chain is woven by a compiler who does the best he can with isolated sayings. The word on causing little ones to stumble (Mk. ix. 42) provides a place for the three sayings on hands, feet, and eyes which cause a man himself to stumble (ix. 43-7). The reference to the fire of Gehenna (ix. 47) leads to the saying, 'Every one shall be salted with fire' (ix. 49), this to the words about salt, and this again to the final saying, 'Have salt in yourselves, and be at peace one with another' (ix. 50).

This kind of artificial arrangement appears to be especially characteristic of the sayings in Mark, but it is also found in some of those which are usually ascribed to Q. A good example is found in the Sermon in Luke where the saying 'Can the blind guide the blind?' is followed by 'The disciple is not above his master', and this by the saying on the Mote and the Beam (vi. 39-42). A still better example is provided by Lk. xvi. 16-8 where three sayings stand together which appear separately in Matthew (xi. 12f., v. 18, 32):

'The law and the prophets were until John: from that time the gospel of the kingdom of God is preached, and every man entereth violently into it.

'But it is easier for heaven and earth to pass away, than for one tittle of the law to fall.

'Every one that putteth away his wife, and marrieth another, committeth adultery: and he that marrieth one that is put away from a husband committeth adultery.'

Since this section is so awkwardly related to its Lukan context, and since it is more likely that Matthew has broken it up than that Luke has put it together, we infer that the complex stood in Q and that this source contained sayings which were artificially compiled. The binding link is the word 'law': and on this slender thread three disparate sayings about the Baptist and the Kingdom, the permanence of the Law, and divorce, are loosely strung together.

Many people do not observe these signs of compilation with pleasure; but the facts are plain, and when they are admitted two valuable results follow. First, we see that mnemonic methods are not new and that the compiler's purpose is didactic; he knows that human memory is weak and so he arranges the sayings in such a way that one suggests and leads on to another. This procedure implies the anxiety of early Christian teachers that the words of Jesus should be remembered; it also implies the existence of communities ready to be taught. In other words, as in the case of the Pronouncement-Stories, testimony is borne to the intense interest of

primitive Christianity in the words of Jesus. The second advantage is not immediately reaped but is of the
greatest importance. This artificial method of arrang-
ing sayings supplies a background against which other
features in the sayings-tradition can be appraised. If
elsewhere in the early collections we find sections which
are not makeshift and artificial in arrangement, we are
driven to ask if they are not the work of an original
mind.

3. Are there sayings-groups where the arrangement
is original? B. S. Easton has not hesitated to say that
'we have every reason to believe that the first tradition of
the sayings-groups and the parables arose in Jesus' life-
time and under His personal direction; the earliest content of the tradition He Himself required His disciples
to commit to memory' (C.G. 41). I must confess that
when first I read these words I thought them too bold;
they seemed to me to represent a view, by no means improbable in itself, which one would readily accept if only
sufficient evidence were forthcoming. But Dr. Easton
has evidence to offer. He reminds us that Jewish
Rabbis used to instruct small groups of intimate disciples, requiring them to memorise their own most important sayings; and he argues that, since Jesus was frequently addressed as 'Rabbi', and had to prepare His
disciples within a brief space of time for popular preaching, it is probable that He used similar methods. Moreover, the 'Mission Charges' in the Gospels take the content of the Message so much for granted that only the
manner of its delivery is described. In addition to
general considerations of this kind Dr. Easton also

shows that sayings-groups in the sources form closely-knit paragraphs, and in this connexion he refers to Lk. vi. 27-38.[1]

Dr. Easton points out that in vv. 27-30 four clauses are balanced by four others and are followed by a summary in v. 31; that the parallel sayings in vv. 32-4 are followed by a similar summary in v. 35; and that the theme of v. 36 receives a fourfold elaboration in vv. 37-8a, while v. 38b is irrelevant to the context (*C.G.* 14). All this is not easy to follow when it is stated baldly, nor is it fully apparent in the prose rendering of the Revised Version; but it becomes clear when the section is written in sense-lines.

27 'Love your enemies,
     Do good to them that hate you,
28 Bless them that curse you,
     Pray for them that despitefully use you.

29 'To him that smiteth thee on the one cheek, offer also the
          other;
     And from him that taketh away thy cloke withhold not
          thy coat also.
30 Give to every one that asketh thee;
     And of him that taketh away thy goods ask them not
          again.

31 'And as ye would that men should do to you,
     Do ye also to them likewise.

32 'And if ye love them that love you,
     What thank have ye?
   For even sinners love them that love them.

---

[1]Easton claims this complex for the L source, but it is usually, and I believe rightly, treated as material from Q. This point, however, is not vital to the argument.

33 And if ye do good to them that do good to you,
        What thank have ye?
    For even sinners do the same.

34 And if ye lend to them of whom ye hope to receive,
        What thank have ye?
    Even sinners lend to sinners, to receive again as much.

35 'But love your enemies, and do them good,
    And lend, hoping for no return;[1]
    (And your reward shall be great),[2]
    And ye shall be sons of the Most High:
    For he is kind toward the unthankful and evil.

36 'Be ye merciful, even as your Father is merciful.

37 'And judge not, and ye shall not be judged:
    And condemn not, and ye shall not be condemned:
    Release, and ye shall be released:

38 Give, and it shall be given unto you;

    'Good measure, pressed down, shaken together, running over,
    Shall they give into your bosom.'

    '(For with what measure ye mete,
    It shall be measured to you again).'[3]

The well-knit character and the poetic form of this section are undeniable, and they leave the impression of originality.   It is true that we cannot on this account alone attribute the section to Jesus; but what other suggestion is as good?   We can hardly trace the Semitic parallelism to the hand of the Gentile Evangelist, and, if it is suggested that it is the work of the compiler of Q, the

[1]So Easton, *St. Luke*, p. 88; Field, *Otium Norv.* iii. 40; Klostermann, *Das Lukasevangelium*, p. 82; Creed, *St. Luke*, p. 94.   On the other hand, see Plummer, *St. Luke*, p. 188.

[2]Apparently an intrusion (? from v. 23).

[3]This couplet appears to be added from another part of Q.   Cf. Mt. vii. 2.   Cf. also Mk. iv. 24.

question why elsewhere his arrangement of the sayings
is as artificial as that of the Markan compiler is not
easily answered.

Albertz (*S.S.* 146-9) has pointed out another primitive unit embedded in Mt. v. 17-48, a section the
greater part of which both Streeter and Bussmann
ascribe to M.   The keynote is given in the opening
words, 'Think not that I came to destroy the law and the
prophets', and the most striking feature is the presence
of six passages which open with the phrase, 'Ye have
heard that it was said to them of old time', or with
similar words.   In three of these passages the foundation principle is perfectly illustrated.   The word of
Jesus stands over against that which was said in the Old
Testament: the Law is not annulled, but it is reinterpreted in a more spiritual direction.   The Law forbade
murder; Jesus condemns anger (21f.): it prohibited
adultery; Jesus forbids lust (27f.): it condemned per-
jury; Jesus puts a ban on the swearing of oaths (33-7).
In contrast with these passages the remaining passages
are structurally imperfect.   In 31f. the law of divorce is
replaced rather than reinterpreted; the *jus talionis*, cited
in 38ff., admittedly stands in the Old Testament, but it
is open to question whether in the time of Jesus it had
not become obsolete (Albertz); in 43ff. the words about
hating enemies do not appear verbatim in the Old Testament at all.   The significant thing is that these three
passages, along with 25f., have all been taken from Q,
and that, when they are removed, the structural form
of the section is more perfect.   This in itself suggests
that the two sources, M and Q, have been used in the

composition of 17-48. Albertz does not suggest that 31f., 38ff., and 43ff. are not genuine sayings of Jesus, but that in Q they did not possess the antithetical form, and that they have this form now because they have been inserted into a context where the antitheses were primitive. The primitive unit, as Albertz sees it, is 17, 21-2a, 27f, 33-4a, 37.

Of this complex he says: 'The connexion of a genuinely conservative attitude with a criticism which goes out from the most inward point bears the stamp of genuineness', and he adds that he sees no reason why the grouping should not already have been completed by Jesus Himself (*S.S.* 148). It must, I think, be admitted that this is source-criticism of a really objective kind. The only questionable element seems to me the omission of 22b and 34b-6, and perhaps also of 18-20.[1]

In 21f, 27f, 33-7, the strophic parallelism is especially notable:

> 21 'Ye have heard that it was said to them of old time,
>   "Thou shalt not kill;
>   And whosoever shall kill
>   Shall be in danger of the judgement":
> 22 But I say unto you,
>   "Every one who is angry with his brother
>   Shall be in danger of the judgement;
>   And whosoever shall say to his brother, 'Raca',
>   Shall be in danger of the council;
>   And whosoever shall say, 'Thou fool',
>   Shall be in danger of the hell of fire".

---

[1] 29f. may well have been added by Matthew from some other part of M, but 22b and 34b-36 seem rather to be in their original context. I cannot see a new point of view in 20 which is other than that of 17. But cf. Albertz, *S.S.* 149.

27 Ye have heard that it was said,
  "Thou shalt not commit adultery":
But I say unto you,
  "Every one that looketh on a woman to lust after her
  Hath committed adultery with her already in his
    heart".

33 Ye have heard that it was said to them of old time,
  "Thou shalt not forswear thyself,
  But shalt perform unto the Lord thine oaths":
34 But I say unto you,
  "Swear not at all.
  Neither by the heaven,
    For it is the throne of God;
35 Nor by the earth,
    For it is the footstool of his feet;
  Nor by Jerusalem,
    For it is the city of the great king.
36 Neither shalt thou swear by thy head,
    For thou canst not make one hair white or black.
37 But let your speech be 'Yea, yea'; 'Nay, nay':
  And whatsoever is more than these is of the evil one".'

Is the inference too bold that the section is a primitive unit to which the First Evangelist has added sayings from Q and M?

It is evident that much work still remains to be done, in order that we may see where isolated sayings have been artificially combined and where original groups have found their way into the tradition. The research student who undertakes this task will need to combine a wide knowledge of detail with sound literary judgment, without which Source-Criticism is degraded to the level of a jig-saw puzzle. There are other places in Q and in M where inquiries like those of Easton and Albertz can

be pushed further. The fourfold structure of Lk. **vi.**
20-6 and the artistic form of Mt. vi. 1-6, 16-8 are examples, and there are others. It is clear that, besides
Pronouncement-Stories and isolated sayings, primitive
groups of sayings were known which, if not susceptible
of absolute identification, are best explained as compositions of Jesus Himself.[1]

II

In addition to the sayings, some account must be
given of the *parables* which formed so rich an element in
early Christian tradition.

In respect of form, the parables are more elaborate
developments of the figures, comparisons, and meta-
phors which are so frequent in the sayings of Jesus.
This is seen at once if we compare characteristic sayings
like those on Wineskins (Mk. ii. 22) and the Mote and
the Beam (Mt. vii. 3ff.):

'No man putteth new wine into old wineskins:
Else the wine will burst the skins,
And the wine perisheth, and the skins:
But they put new wine into fresh wineskins.'

'Why beholdest thou the mote that is in thy brother's eye,
But considerest not the beam that is in thine own eye?
Or how wilt thou say to thy brother,
"Let me cast out the mote out of thine eye";
And lo, the beam is in thine own eye?'

Since the classical discussion of parables in Jülicher's
Die Gleichnisreden Jesu (1899) it has been usual to dis-

[1] Cf. T. W. Manson: 'Perhaps we should regard this strophic parallelism, as the most distinctive characteristic of his poetry and his special
contribution to the forms of poetry in general' (*T.J.* 56).

tinguish between the Similitude, the Parable, and the
Illustrative Story. The Similitude is distinguished
from the comparison by the detail of the picture; the
Parable from the Similitude by the presence of a narrative which serves as a comparison, or presents an interesting individual case rather than a typical circumstance;
the Illustrative Story from the Parable by the fact that
the moral lies in the narrative itself. These distinctions
are easy to make, and for the most part can be readily
applied, but difficulties arise in certain cases. For example, are the Hid Treasure and the Pearl Merchant
Similitudes or Parables? Such questions can hardly be
answered unless we know the Speaker's intentions, and
the form itself does not always permit us to know these.
Similarly, the bounds between Parables and Illustrative
Stories are fleeting, but the clearest examples of the
latter are the four Lukan stories of the Good Samaritan,
the Rich Fool, the Rich Man and Lazarus, and the
Pharisee and the Publican. It is of the essence of the
Parable that it suggests an analogy to a spiritual truth;
the point is not in the details nor in the quality of the actions described. Neglect of this principle has played
havoc with the exegesis of parables, especially those in
Luke. Neither the man who does not want to leave his
bed nor the judge who seeks to escape further trouble is
the God to whom we pray: the point of both parables is
the need for perseverance in prayer. Nor is God the
oriental master of whom Jesus asks: 'Doth he thank the
servant because he did the things that were commanded?'
The teaching is that, when we have done all these
things, we have to say: 'We are unprofitable servants;

we have done that which it was our duty to do' (Lk. xvii. 10).

It is evident from the Gospels that the parables circulated singly or in pairs, and that collections were made at different centres. The introductions are for the most part added by the Evangelists, and are derived from the parables themselves. So, too, there is a tendency, which can be observed in the parable of the Unjust Steward, to add sayings of a similar character. The effect of this, as Bultmann points out, is to introduce an element of uncertainty into the interpretation of parables. Both the Friend at Midnight and the Unjust Judge are parables which teach the duty of prayer, but prayer for what? Is it a matter of prayer in general or of prayer for the inbreaking of the Kingdom? The Unjust Steward teaches that the saints may learn from the trickery of a knave, but in what direction? These problems meet us at every turn, but it would be wrong to suggest that they throw exegesis as a whole into hopeless confusion. As a rule the meaning is reasonably clear, and where this is not so the parables fulfil a purpose which Jesus intended in provoking deeper thought on the problems of life and of faith.

The question whether Jesus made use of Allegory has long been a burning issue. Here Bultmann takes sides with Jülicher and against Fiebig in maintaining that instances of allegory are due to later Christian reflection, but he admits that Jülicher found traces which do not really exist, as in the references to the king in the parable of the Talents (Mt. xviii. 23) and the lender in the Two Debtors (Lk. vii. 41). The interpretations which are added to the Sower (Mk. iv. 13-20), and the Tares (Mt. xiii. 36-43) are widely, and rightly, understood as primitive Christian expositions, and this, not because Jewish teachers did not add explanations in response to the requests of their disciples (cf. Fiebig, *E.E.* 52), but because the expositions miss the point of the parables and appear to be adapted to later interests and conditions. On the general question, whether Jesus ever used allegorical methods, we ought not to take a hard and fast view, but to recognize that, while it was not His custom to do so, He did on occasion press details in parables, as, for example, in the Wicked Husbandmen (Mk. xii. 1-11), in a pointed way which hearers would understand.[1]

In recent years the industry of P. Fiebig,[2] and of H. L. Strack and P. Billerbeck,[3] has greatly added to our knowledge of Jewish parables. I fear I can reproduce here only two of the examples which Bultmann cites (*G.S.T.* 218).

'Be not like servants who serve their master under the condition that they receive a reward, but rather like servants who serve their master under the condition that they receive no reward' (*Pirké Aboth*, I. 3; cf. Lk. xvii. 7-10).

'Every one whose wisdom is greater than his deeds, to whom is he like? To a tree which has many branches, but whose roots are few; and the wind comes and uproots it and overturns it. But every one whose deeds are greater than his wisdom, to whom is he like? To a tree which has few branches, and whose roots

---

[1]See further the excellent article by W. J. Moulton on Parable in *D.C.G.* ii. 312-7.

[2]*Altjüdische Gleichnisse und die Gleichnisse Jesu* (1904).

[3]*Kommentar zum N. T. aus Talmud und Midrasch*, i.-iv. 1922-8.

are many, so that, even if all winds in the world should come and blow upon it, it could not be moved away from its place' (*Pirkê Aboth*, III. 18; cf. Mt. vii. 24-7).

Bultmann says that the kindredship with the Jewish Similitudes may simply mean that Jesus 'stood in the Jewish tradition and, as a man of His time and of His people, formed Similitudes like the men of His time and country' (*G.S.T.* 219f.); but he raises the question whether parables from the Jewish tradition may not have been ascribed to Jesus by the community. Apart, however, from a few parables like Lk. xvi. 19-31, he does not press this suggestion far, and would, I think, have given it less weight if he had developed his observation that 'Jesus Himself could have taken up a current story' (*G.S.T.* 222).

The Illustrative Stories are especially interesting, and it is not surprising that attempts have been made to find current tales on which they have been based. Gressmann, for example, gives striking parallels in Egyptian and Jewish sources to the first part of the Rich Man and Lazarus (Lk. xvi. 19-31). Setne, the son of Rameses II., sees the burial of a rich and a poor man, and declares how much better the rich fare in death than the poor. Whereupon, Horus, his divine Son, shows him the fortunes of the two in the nether-world, the poor man royally clad in linen and the rich man wearing the grave clothes of the pauper. Gressmann suggests that Jesus has reshaped the popular story, but has added the scene in 27-31 which teaches that not even the return of a man from Hades will convert those who are unresponsive to Moses and the prophets. Naturally, all theories of the

kind must be speculative, and in the present case the
parallels may be accidental.   But even if the connexion
is real, the originality of Jesus is no more impugned
than is the genius of Shakespeare when tales are found
on which his plots are based.   Indeed, the suggestion is
attractive that Jesus took details from folklore and from
contemporary history (cf. Lk. xix. 12, 27) and wove
them into immortal stories which convey their own les-
son without need of commentary or learned explanation.

III

Having examined the formal aspects of the sayings
and parables I now turn more directly to the question of
their genuineness.   I have suggested that the forms indicate that the tradition has been preserved with considerable fidelity; but, of course, this question must be discussed on broader lines.   Two questions in particular
claim attention: (1) Is the tradition substantially trustworthy?; (2) To what extent, and from what causes has
it suffered in the course of transmission?   In discussing
these questions it will be useful to have in mind the
views of Bultmann.

Bultmann, we have seen, thinks that the tradition has
received many modifications and additions, and that
many of the sayings are really 'Christian formations'.
Only in a few cases, he holds, can we have any confidence
in ascribing individual Logia to Jesus (G.S.T. 110),
since many of them may well be popular sayings of
Jewish and oriental origin.   The sayings which are
most likely to be genuine are those which reveal a
strongly marked eschatological attitude or the energy of

the call to repentance, or those which demand a new attitude or commend non-resistance (Mt. v. 39*b*-41) and the love of enemies (Mt. v. 44-8). Of these passages and others like Mk. iii. 27 (the strong man), vii. 15 (things that defile), viii. 35 (On saving one's life), and x. 15 (On receiving the Kingdom as a child), he says: 'All these words . . . contain something characteristic, new, which goes beyond popular wisdom and piety, and yet is just as little specifically scribal and rabbinical or Jewish-apocalyptic' (*G.S.T.* 110). As may be supposed, he gives more favourable judgment to the prophetic and apocalyptic sayings by which Jesus proclaims the in-breaking of the Kingdom and calls men to righteousness (Mt. xi. 5f., Lk. vi. 20f., x. 23); but, again, many of these passages are rejected as 'Christian formations'. Among the latter are Mk. ix. 1 ('There be some here'), xiii. 31 ('Heaven and earth shall pass'), and Lk. xii. 32 ('Fear not, little flock'). Even Mk. xiii. 32 ('Of that day'), one of Schmiedel's 'pillar-passages', comes under the axe. In like manner, many of the sayings about the Law, and 'community-rules' like Mt. xvi. 18f. (Peter) and xviii. 18 (Binding and loosing) are traced to 'debates' within the Palestinian community, while most of the sayings in the first person singular are looked upon as 'a work of the Hellenistic community'. The parables are treated with surprising caution (cf. Fascher, *F.M.* 120).

It is evident that I have done Bultmann no injustice in speaking of his regard for possibilities: no tendency which conceivably might have corrupted the tradition is missed; no power of the mind to forget, to transform,

and to create is neglected. For Bultmann, the personality of Jesus is faint and remote; but the community is
alert, full-blooded, ready for every enterprise of corruption and creation. I have no doubt that he lays a just
finger on tendencies which do darken the tradition; but
several considerations show that his position as a whole
is one of violent exaggeration.

1. In the first place, as I observed in the second lecture, Bultmann takes no account of the existence of eyewitnesses. The orphaned Christian community has no
leaders to whom it can appeal for an account of what
Jesus said: it might have been marooned on an island in
the Greek Archipelago! This attitude is due to Bultmann's preoccupation with forms, but it vitiates a study
of the question of genuineness from the beginning.

2. Again, the creative power of the community is too
easily assumed. Do communities produce matchless
sayings like those of Jesus? Easton rightly maintains
that sayings are created by individuals, not by communities. 'Communities', he says, 'may adopt and transmit
sayings, and may modify and standardize them in transmission, but the sayings themselves must first exist'
(*G.G.* 116).

3. Further, the theory of extensive 'Christian formations' does not at all harmonize with the actual conditions of the primitive period. The first Christians were
much more alive to the distinction between what Jesus
had said and what He had not said than Bultmann al-
lows. In I Cor. vii. Paul clearly distinguishes between
his own commands and those which had been given by
Christ (vv. 10, 12); he speaks also of matters in respect

of which he has 'no commandment of the Lord' (vv. 25, 40).   What an opportunity for a 'Christian formation'! Bultmann himself supplies an example which tells in the opposite direction from the one he favours.   He suggests that words like Apoc. xvi. 15 ('Behold, I come as a thief') were gradually carried over to the historical Jesus and treated as words of His.   This is a plausible suggestion, until we observe that in the Apocalypse, written at the end of the first century, such words are still taken for what they are—words of the Exalted Christ speaking through the lips of Christian prophets.   The presumption is that the community knew the difference between such utterances and those of the historical Jesus.

4. Objection must also be taken to the way in which parallels are overworked, and to the suggestion that Jewish tradition was ascribed to Jesus.   If this were offered as a possibility, to be suspected here and there, no one could reasonably object; nor would the error be serious, since a saying could be mistakenly attributed to Him only because it was *in character*, and accordant with His teaching as a whole.   But the more numerous such cases are said to be, the less innocent they are, until the community becomes directly responsible for the errors, a possibility which is strongly opposed by the considerations I have just urged.

5. Finally, Bultmann's tests of genuineness are much too subjective.   Can we get very far by selecting a few characteristic features in the sayings of Jesus, and by making these a touchstone by which we decide the genuineness of the tradition as a whole?   To decide what is characteristic is not easy, and, even if we can do

this, the test must often fail because even the greatest of teachers often say familiar things.   Great teachers refuse to be true to type, even their own type.   Bultmann looks with favour on eschatological sayings and on words which call men to repentance and moral decision.   In this he is right, but the preference supplies no principle by which we may exclude other sayings; it does not help us to hear the voice of the community.   What is wanted is some more objective test, such as that supplied by B. S. Easton.   In the course of an invaluable discussion of the Synoptic Perspective, Easton makes a list of tenets which were held by the first church but were either not part of the message of Jesus or were rarely taught by Him.   He shows how scantily these tenets are supported by sayings ascribed to Jesus, and concludes that the primary historic value of the Synoptists is for the tradition of the teaching of Jesus, not for the age in which they were written (*G.G.* p. 109).   This is an objective test and its results point to the substantial trustworthiness of the sayings-tradition.

These criticisms supply an answer to the first question.   But to them we must add the considerations suggested by our own study of forms.   The parallelism of the sayings suggests their Palestinian character.   The artificiality of some of the groupings suggests that compilers are dealing with given material, not with plastic forms.   The structure of other sayings-groups points to the work of a creative mind other than that of the compilers of sources or the Evangelists.   To these arguments we must add a consideration which is not capable of scientific proof, but which becomes stronger in its effect upon the mind the longer the sayings and parables are studied. There is in the great majority of the sayings attributed to Jesus a self-authenticating note which stamps them as His, and not the formations of the community. This is an aesthetic judgment, and its limits cannot be precisely fixed, but it ought not to be neglected by any one who seeks to give a comprehensive opinion on the historical value of the sayings. Taken along with the more objective arguments, it confirms our conclusion that substantially the sayings-tradition is historically trustworthy.

I pass now to the second question: To what extent and from what causes has the tradition suffered in the course of transmission?

The answer just given to the first question does not preclude this further inquiry, for it is impossible to prove inerrancy for the sayings-tradition, and the probabilities are all against it. The extent to which the tradition has suffered will be variously estimated by different investigators. In view of my previous discussion I do not think it is far-reaching in its range, but it is certainly a factor to be taken into serious account. It is of greater importance, however, to examine the causes which are responsible for the obscuring of the original tradition, and these I will now indicate.

1. In the first place, most of the sayings must have been spoken in Aramaic, whereas we have them now in Greek; and translation, however faithful, must always mean some loss of accuracy and the possibility of error. Proved cases of mistranslation naturally cannot be given; the best suggested example is that of Wellhausen, who

thinks that Luke's rendering: 'Give for alms those
things which are within' (xi. 41) as compared with that
of Mt. xxiii. 26: 'Cleanse first the inside of the cup', is
due to a translator who read the Aramaic דַּכִּי (dakki),
'purify', as if it were זַכִּי (zakki), 'give alms'.

2. Again, there are cases where a saying is modified
by the context in which it appears.   For example, Luke
records the saying (xii. 3):

'Whatsoever ye have said in the darkness
Shall be heard in the light;
And what ye have spoken in the ear in the inner chambers
Shall be proclaimed upon the housetops.'

Here the meaning is that which is expressed by the
proverb, 'Truth will out'.   But in Mt. x. 27 the same
saying appears with the meaning, 'Tell what you have
been told': 'What I tell you in the darkness,
Speak ye in the light:
And what ye hear in the ear,
Proclaim upon the housetops.'

When we see that the theme of Mt. x. is the Mission
Charge to the Twelve, it seems plain that Matthew has
adapted the saying to this context.

3. Further, a saying may be modified by religious interests.   The phrase 'Son of man', for example, may be
introduced into a context to which it does not belong.
We can see that this has happened when we compare an
earlier and a later Gospel: in Mk. viii. 27 Jesus asks:
'Who do men say that I am?'; but in Mt. xvi. 13 the
question appears in the form: 'Who do men say that the
Son of man is?'   It is probable that the same thing has

happened in the saying about blasphemy against the Son of man (Lk. xii. 10 = Mt. xii. 32); the Markan form of the saying speaks of blasphemy against 'the sons of men' (iii. 28).

4. More debatable are the cases in which sayings have been modified by later dogmatic beliefs, by controversies, or by existing practices. The development of belief probably accounts for the trinitarian language of Mt. xxviii. 19 where baptism is commanded 'into the name of the Father and of the Son and of the Holy Spirit', since, according to Acts viii. 16, the first Christians appear to have been baptized 'into the name of the Lord Jesus'. It may be, as many suppose, that the words addressed to Peter in Mt. xvi. 18ff. have been influenced by controversies between parties in the Infant Church; and there is reason to think that the command to 'make disciples of all the nations' has been shaped by experiences in the Gentile Mission, since otherwise we cannot understand the hesitation of the first Christians to embark on the task of world-evangelization. From sayings of this kind it is easy to draw the erroneous conclusion that the tradition of the words of Jesus is quite uncertain, and that we cannot be sure of anything He is reported to have said. This view, however, can be held only by neglecting the larger considerations I have previously mentioned. Such a conclusion also ignores the fact that by critical methods it is often possible to reduce, and even to remove, the measure of uncertainty. Very many of the sayings are given by two Evangelists, and some by three, and a careful comparison of different versions often enables us to decide which

of them more truly represents the actual words of Jesus; and even where a saying occurs once only, we can compare it with what we otherwise know of the teaching of Jesus and form an opinion of its genuineness.   It is, however, idle to deny that there are sayings about which we are compelled to hesitate.   Personally, I do not think that there are many sayings of the kind, and I have no hesitation in claiming that the tradition of the words of Jesus is far better preserved than we have any right to expect, and with much greater accuracy than is to be found in the record of the words of any great teacher of the past.

IV

No study of the sayings of Jesus is complete which does not consider those recorded in the Fourth Gospel; and indeed in an investigation of the formation of the Gospel tradition such an inquiry is indispensable.   The subject, however, is so difficult that I fear I can do no more than indicate conclusions to which the evidence appears to point.[1]

1.   It is not possible to regard the Johannine sayings as a whole as verbatim accounts of what Jesus actually said.   The difference between these sayings and those in the Synoptic Gospels is too great, while the same type of utterance reappears in the Prologue to the Fourth Gospel, the speeches of the Baptist, and in the Johannine Epistles.   These facts suggest that we have to allow for an element which comes from the Evangelist

[1] I have discussed various aspects of this subject in three articles in the *Hibbert Journal*, xxv. 740-3, xxvii. 123-37, xxviii. 531-46.

H

himself. It is important, however, not to exaggerate the difference between the Johannine and the Synoptic sayings. Even in the latter there is sometimes an element of interpretation, and the Fourth Gospel probably contains sayings which closely reproduce what Jesus said. Examples of these are reasonably to be found in such pithy sayings as: 'My meat is to do the will of him that sent me'; 'Work not for the meat which perisheth, but for the meat which abideth unto eternal life'; 'Greater love hath no man than this, that a man lay down his life for his friends'; and in other passages of like kind.

2. On the other hand, it is very improbable that the Johannine sayings are inventions pure and simple. Such an explanation is not in harmony with the writer's purpose as expressed in the words: 'These are written, that ye may believe that Jesus is the Christ, the Son of God; and that believing ye may have life in his name' (xx. 31). Moreover, many Johannine sayings re-echo Synoptic utterances in another idiom,[1] and others are so true to current Rabbinical thought, and so lifelike, that a Jewish scholar like Dr. Israel Abrahams writes: 'My own general impression, without asserting an early date for the Fourth Gospel, is that that Gospel enshrines a genuine tradition of an aspect of Jesus' teaching which has not found a place in the Synoptics'.[2]

3. Only a partial explanation is found in the suggestion that the Fourth Gospel portrays the thoughts of

[1]Cf. W. F. Howard, *The Fourth Gospel in Recent Criticism and Interpretation*, 1931, pp. 215-29.

[2]*Studies in Pharisaism and the Gospels*, 1st series, 1917, p. 12.

Jesus in the same way that the writings of Plato express the thoughts of Socrates.   With all his veneration for Socrates, Plato did not proclaim him as divine, nor did he ask for faith in his name.   Nor again, was he anxious to insist that he was a real person who had appeared in flesh and blood.   With every desire to reinterpret the primitive tradition, the Fourth Evangelist had definite historical interests at stake, and these could not be met by merely voicing the thoughts of Jesus.   For this reason his task can only very partially be compared with that of a modern novelist who seeks to recreate the past.

4. If we want to understand the Johannine sayings we must allow for the influence of the Evangelist's spiritual environment, and above all for his Christian experience.   The strength of his experience is evident from the Gospel itself and from the Epistles which come from his pen.   The character of his religious environment is seen when we read the parallel sayings which, with the greatest industry, have been gathered from all quarters in the writings of Philo, the *Odes of Solomon*, the Hermetic writings, and the sacred books of Mandaism. Most of the evidence is later than the Evangelist's time; none the less, it discloses forms of expression which have a long history behind them, and which may well have served him as vehicles of expression.   Ideas of mediation and references to the despatch of divine envoys from heaven to earth would appeal to his mind because there was much that was analogous to them in the story and message of Jesus; and such thoughts would inevitably colour the sayings as he remembered them.   The environment of thought is more subtle than the environ-

ment of circumstance; we remember things and express
them in terms of what we know and like. The savage
can often repeat a message in the exact words in which it
is given to him; for the man of culture and deep feeling
this is generally impossible. Where verbal reproduction is the one essential, he is the last person to be en-
trusted with a message. He cannot transmit it without
interpretation; what he tells is not that which he is told,
but the message after it has passed through the fires of
his thought, imagination, and experience. Such a process is not loss when it takes place in the mind of a writer
like the Fourth Evangelist. Different in form, the final
result may be a truer representation of the original saying because elements are brought out which were latent
or but partially expressed.

5. Several scholars have urged that the Jewish practice of Targuming presents the best analogy.[1] When
the Rabbi translated the sacred words of the Law from
Hebrew to Aramaic he by no means always gave a literal
translation of the original; sometimes the version would
be free, and at other times a definite element of interpretation would enter into the rendering. He would have
been shocked, however, at the charge that he was falsi-
fying the Word; he would have replied that he was con-
veying its true meaning. Such is the method of the
Fourth Evangelist; he begins with words of Jesus, but
he is not a mouthpiece. Year after year he has pondered the sayings, seeing deeper and deeper meaning in

[1]Cf. E. A. Abbott, *The Son of Man*, 1910, p. 411; H. A. A. Kennedy,
Philo's Contribution to Religion, 1919, 50f.; W. F. Howard, *The Fourth
Gospel in Recent Criticism and Interpretation*, 1931, 226-9.

them. The result is that when he takes up his pen to
write, some of the sayings are words of Jesus transposed
into another key, and others are new formations which
have grown out of original utterances and have extended
them in new directions. The Evangelist himself cannot have been ignorant of this, for it was his ardent belief
that the Spirit would bring to Christ's disciples all that
He had said to them (xiv. 26). He cannot possibly
have thought of this as a mechanical process; something
vital is implied when he writes: 'Howbeit when he, the
Spirit of truth, is come, he shall guide you into all the
truth' (xvi. 13). We must therefore conclude that he
was conscious of the difference between his Gospel and
the Synoptic tradition of the words of Jesus, and that he
believed that he was guided by the Spirit in his work of
interpretation. It is possible that he would not have
admitted the human element which we can see when we
read his Gospel; he believed himself to be guided by the
Spirit; he was telling his readers what Jesus had really
said, a truth more glorious than anything contained in
the Synoptic tradition. Such was his belief, and the
place which his book occupies in the affections and
esteem of the Catholic Church shows that in a large
measure he has succeeded. Least historical in the nar-
rower sense of the word, it is the most historical of all,
because here more than anywhere else we read the secret
of the significance of Jesus. Not all critics accept this
estimate, but I believe that it is the one which does most
justice to the Gospel, its history in the life of the Church,
and its power over the individual mind.

God's gifts are costly; and the price of His gift in the

Fourth Gospel is that we cannot tell where the Master's words pass into the Evangelist's idiom. But if we cannot escape this embarrassment, we can surmount it in gratitude for a gift which exceeds in value the report of a stenographer. Perhaps the lines of Browning express the truth best, when he asks if the Yellow Book really existed or whether his story is just make-belief, and says that it contains:

> 'Something of mine which, mixed up with the mass,
> Made it bear hammer and be firm to file.'

The Evangelist would have said this of the Spirit, and with reference to the Synoptic tradition: he truly had given the words of Jesus in his Gospel, and the words were 'spirit and life' because they were the utterances of Jesus as the Spirit revealed them to him.

VI

THE MIRACLE-STORIES

IN many respects the Miracle-Stories raise the most difficult problems which meet us in connexion with the Gospel tradition, and it is important that they should be treated with complete frankness. Unfortunately, however, this quality is often too narrowly understood. There is the frankness of those who are prepared to defend the miracles of the Gospels against all comers; and there is the frankness of those who leave us in no doubt about their wholehearted rejection of the miraculous. There is, however, another manner of approach which is bent less on winning a verdict than on facing all the facts of the case, and which leads the inquirer to accept conclusions when the evidence is clear, and also to confess ignorance and uncertainty when unknown factors are met. This is the kind of frankness I desire to display in the present lecture.

I have already included among the Pronouncement-Stories three narratives which record miracles: the Man with the Withered Hand, the Bent Woman, and the Dropsical Man; and I have also referred to the possibility that the Syro-Phoenician Woman, the Centurion's Servant, and the Ten Lepers may originally have belonged to this class. These are not Miracle-Stories proper, because the miracle is not the main point of interest, but rather some saying or attitude of Jesus to moral and religious questions. These stories do not immediately concern us; they have, however, a close bearing on the subject, because the incidental way in which they tell of 'mighty works' is the best of evidence that Jesus wrought them; and the same is true of the words in the Beelzebub Controversy: 'If I by the finger of God cast out devils, then is the kingdom of God come upon you' (Lk. xi. 20 = Mt. xii. 28).

The Miracle-Stories proper include thirteen healing-miracles and five nature-miracles. The former include: the Demoniac in the Synagogue, Peter's Wife's Mother, the Leper, the Paralytic, the Gerasene Demoniac, the Daughter of Jaïrus, the Woman with the Issue, the Deaf Mute, the Blind Man near Bethsaida, the Epileptic Lad, Blind Bartimaeus,[1] the Dumb Demoniac (Lk. xi. 14 = Mt. xii. 22-4; cf. ix. 32-4), and the Young Man at Nain (Lk. vii. 11-7). The nature-miracles are the Stilling of the Storm, the Feeding of the Five Thousand, the Walking on the Water, the Cursing of the Fig Tree, and the Draught of Fishes.[2] The two stories which are peculiar to the Fourth Gospel, the Changing of Water into Wine (ii. 1-11) and the Raising of Lazarus (xi. 1-46), probably presuppose earlier popular forms, but their precise character during the oral period cannot now be determined, and for this reason they are not treated in the present lecture.

[1]The first eleven are Markan stories: i. 23-7; i. 30f.; i. 40-5; ii. 1-12; v. 1-20; v. 21-43; v. 25-34; vii. 32-7; viii. 22-6; ix. 14-29; x. 46-52.

[2]Mk. iv. 35-41; vi. 34-44 (cf. viii. 1-9); vi. 45-52; xi. 13f.; Lk. v. 1-11.

I

Our first task must be to examine the form or forms in which Miracle-Stories appear in the Gospels.

In my second lecture I accepted the Miracle-Story as a popular narrative form with special features of its own. This view, I think, will be confirmed by our present study; but it will also appear that important qualifications have to be made, and that distinctions other than those between healing- and nature-miracles need to be drawn.

All the elements of a popular oral story are found in the Demoniac in the Synagogue at Capernaum (Mk. i. 23-7). First, the circumstances are described—the teaching in the synagogue and the presence of the demoniac who perceives and resents the presence of the Healer.

'What have we to do with thee, thou Jesus of Nazareth? art thou come to destroy us? I know thee who thou art, the Holy One of God.'

Then the healing is recorded:

'And Jesus rebuked him, saying, "Hold thy peace, and come out of him". And the unclean spirit, tearing him and crying with a loud voice, came out of him.'

Finally, the impression produced on the onlookers is described:

'And they were all amazed, insomuch that they questioned among themselves, saying, "What is this? . . . with authority he commandeth even the unclean spirits, and they obey him".'

Even in a brief story like that of Peter's Wife's Mother (Mk. i. 29-31) the same form appears, except that instead of a reference to the effect produced, a con-

firmation of the cure is supplied in the statement that
'she ministered unto them'.   In the story of the Leper
(Mk. i. 40-5), the form is present to perfection, with the
addition that here, as in the Deaf Mute (Mk. vii. 32-7),
the Blind Man near Bethsaida (Mk. viii. 22-6), and the
Daughter of Jaïrus (Mk. v. 21-4, 35-43), a charge to
maintain silence is given, which, since the time of
Wrede, has so often and so unconvincingly been attributed to the Evangelist.   The common form also appears in the story of the Paralytic (Mk. ii. 3-5a, 10b-2).
Here the circumstances are more fully described.   Unable to reach the presence of Jesus, the four bearers
break up the roof and let down the paralytic on his
pallet.   Jesus heals with a word, and confirmation follows in the departure of the man carrying his bed, while
the astonishment of the crowd is voiced in the cry: 'We
never saw it on this fashion'.

Already to some extent in the story of the Paralytic,
and still more in the account of the Gerasene Demoniac
(Mk. v. 1-20), an increase in the amount of detail becomes noticeable.   How realistic is the description of
the demoniac:

'a man with an unclean spirit, who had his dwelling in the tombs:
and no man could any more bind him, no, not with a chain; because that he had been often bound with fetters and chains, and
the chains had been rent asunder by him, and the fetters broken in
pieces: and no man had strength to tame him.   And always,
night and day, in the tombs and in the mountains, he was crying
out, and cutting himself with stones'!

The roughness of this description relieves the story of
the charge of literary embellishment; while the amount

of detail forbids us to suppose that we have here a mere product of the community. This impression deepens as the story proceeds. Like the demoniac at Capernaum, the man perceives and fears the power of Jesus, but the dialogue is more fully reported, and there is a strange yet realistic interplay between the personality cf the man and the spirits by which he believes himself to be possessed. A necessary reference to the part of the story which concerns the swine may for the present be postponed. Meantime, we may note, as formal elements to which hitherto we have had no parallel, the change of scene to the city and the introduction of the men of the district who are afraid and beg Jesus to depart. The result of the cure is given in the picture of the former demoniac 'clothed and in his right mind', but is still further emphasized by the man's request to accompany Jesus and by the command to tell his friends the great things the Lord had done for him, and how He had mercy on him. The question arises whether a story of this kind is rightly classified along with those already considered, and, although similar narratives cannot here be discussed in the same detail, the same question forces itself on the mind in the stories of the Daughter of Jaïrus, the Woman with the Issue (Mk. v. 21-43), and the Epileptic Lad (Mk. ix. 14-29), and, among the Nature-Miracles, in the stories of the Stilling of the Storm (Mk. iv. 35-41), the Feeding of the Five Thousand (Mk. vi. 34-44), and the Walking on the Water (Mk. vi. 45-52). All these are popular stories, but do they not stand appreciably nearer to the accounts of eye-witnesses?

This conviction has often been expressed, but it has been deepened in my own mind by a series of experiments designed to illustrate the tendencies of oral transmission.[1]

The purpose of the experiments was to show what happens when a story containing a good deal of detail is set going in a community, and is recorded at different stages in the course of its transmission. It may be readily allowed that such experiments cannot exactly reproduce the circumstances of the primitive Christian communities; but, on the other hand, some of the disabilities cancel one another. For instance, while the hearers at once wrote down their recollections, each was entirely dependent on his predecessor; and in this way an advantage making for accuracy was checked by a limited channel of information. I submit, therefore, that broad inferences from such tests are permissible. The results are of great interest. The experiments show that the tendency of oral transmission is definitely in the direction of *abbreviation*. Additions are certainly made in all good faith through misunderstandings and efforts to picture the course of events, but almost always the stories become shorter and more conventional. The best analogy is that of pebbles on the seashore which are made smaller and round by the ceaseless beat of the waves.

Such experiments suggest that longer Miracle-Stories, which are not products of literary art, stand near the records of eyewitnesses, and that the shorter and more conventional stories have passed through many hands

[1]See Appendix B.

before they were committed to writing. This distinction cuts right across the classification of healing- and nature-miracles, for it leads us to group together, as stories which stand nearer to original accounts, such narratives as the Gerasene Demoniac, the Daughter of Jaïrus, the Epileptic Lad, the Stilling of the Storm, the Feeding of the Five Thousand, and perhaps the Walking on the Water. On the other hand, a story like the Young Man at Nain (Lk. vii. 11-7) shows distinct signs of weathering, and must have passed through several, and perhaps many, stages of transmission before Luke used and embellished it. If this is so, it is obviously wrong, on formal grounds, to group all the Miracle-Stories together: all are popular forms, but we see them at different stages on the stream of Gospel tradition.

These distinctions, suggested by the form of the stories, bear on the historical question, but they do not enable us to decide that question. The shorter stories are clearly old stories, but their smooth and rounded form puts us at a disadvantage when we ask what it was that really happened. We are in a much more favourable position when we examine the longer stories, for we stand, as it were, nearer to the original events. We cannot, however, assume that the incidents took place just as they are related; indeed, this would not be possible if we possessed the affidavits of actual eyewitnesses. The historical problem still remains open. Nevertheless, the formal distinction is valuable, not only because it indicates the narratives from which the problem may be approached with greater advantage, but also because it shows why that approach is best.

One caveat, already indicated by the reference to literary art, needs to be emphasized. Length and detail alone will not indicate a primitive story, otherwise we might so describe the account of the Raising of Lazarus (Jn. xi. 1-46). Only where details are not due to literary activity and are not subservient to doctrinal interests, can we be sure that we have to do with primitive stories.

II

Having considered the form of the Miracle-Stories, we must now ask if anything is to be learnt from parallel stories in Jewish and Hellenistic tradition. The researches of Weinreich and Fiebig leave us in no doubt that in external respects the parallels are remarkably close. This is evident, for example, in each of the three parts which constitute the form of the New Testament stories. In the Introduction, or 'Exposition', it is common to emphasize the difficulty of the cure by speaking of the duration of the illness, its dangerous character, the failure of previous attempts to effect a cure, the doubt or scorn displayed by the onlookers towards the Healer. All these features can be matched outside the Gospel stories. The same is true of many points connected with the miracle itself. In non-Christian stories use is made of spittle, the healer stands over the sick man, touches him, or takes hold of his hand. Use is made of commanding words, or of words in a strange language, or again an appeal is made to potent names. As in the Gospel narratives the demon perceives the presence of his master and recognizes his power. The exorcist and the demon converse, and the latter begs

favours or demands a right. Finally, in the description
of the result common features are found. Sometimes a
demonstration confirms the reality of the cure. The
departure of the demon, for example, is proved by the
overturning of a vessel of water (Jos. *Antiq*. viii. 2, 5), or
by the overturning of a statue (*Vit. Apol*. iv. 20). The
impression produced on the public is described and the
words of wonder by which the cure is greeted are given.

One of the most interesting of the parallel stories is
told of Apollonius of Tyana.

'A girl had died just in the hour of her marriage, and the
bridegroom was following her bier lamenting as was natural his
marriage left unfulfilled, and the whole of Rome was mourning
with him, for the maiden belonged to a consular family. Apollonius then, witnessing their grief, said: "Put down the bier, for I
will stay the tears that you are shedding for this maiden". And
withal he asked what was her name....Merely touching her and
whispering in secret some spell over her, (he) at once woke up the
maiden from her seeming death; and the girl spoke out loud and
returned to her father's house, just as Alcestis did when she was
brought back to life by Hercules.'[1]

No one, I think, can read this story without being reminded of the Young Man at Nain. It is of interest to
note that the chronicler adds just the kind of comment
which modern readers of the New Testament miracles
frequently make.

'Now whether he detected some spark of life in her, which
those who were nursing her had not noticed—for it is said that,
although it was raining at the time, a vapour went up from her
face—or whether life was really extinct, and he restored it by the

---

[1]Philostratus, *Vita Apollonii*, iv. 45 (Conybeare's translation).

warmth of his touch, is a mysterious problem which neither I myself nor those who were present could decide.'

The parallels are real; but the more important question is 'What do they signify?' Bultmann's answer is that they illustrate the atmosphere, show the *motifs* and forms, and thus help us to understand the entrance of Miracle-Stories into the Gospel tradition (*G.S.T.* 253). He admits that historical events lie at the basis of a few of the healing miracles, but claims that nevertheless their formation is the work of the tradition. Old Testament influences have played their part, and some of the stories have originated within the Christian community itself, but for the most part their origin is to be sought in the influence of popular stories and *motifs*, partly in Palestine, but predominantly on Hellenistic soil (*G.S.T.* 241-256). This seems to me to be a conclusion which altogether outruns the evidence. Koehler, I suggest, gives the true significance of the parallels when he asks: 'Do they not primarily prove merely this, which is not at all new, that healing stories are everywhere narrated in the same manner, because they everywhere take pretty much the same course?' (*F.P.* 37). 'A healing', he adds, and the obvious remark is not out of place, 'is not unhistorical because it has parallels' (*ib.*).

More, however, can be said than this. The parallels collected with so much industry have the effect of displaying the distinctiveness of the stories associated with Jesus. This is shown when Bultmann endorses suggestions which can only be described as 'thin'; as, for example, when he approves of the view that the uncovering of the roof in Mk. ii. 4 goes back to the idea that the right way into the house must remain concealed from the demon (*G.S.T.* 237). It is more clearly evident in the absence from the Gospels of details in non-Christian stories which Bultmann supplies. On rare occasions Jesus uses spittle, but where does He bring a piece from the gravestone of a virgin to a diseased foot or draw out demons by means of a ring?[1] In the story of the Epileptic Lad the youth is left 'as one dead' (Mk. ix. 26), but where in the Gospels do demons prove their departure by overturning vessels of water or by smashing statues (cf. *G.S.T.* 240)? Only in the case of the destruction of the swine have we a partial parallel (cf. Mk. v. 11-3), and this is capable of a natural explanation which does not compromise the reality of the cure.

One of the most frequently quoted parallels is that supplied by Josephus in the *Antiquities* (viii. 2, 5).

'I have seen a certain man of my own country whose name was Eleazer, releasing people that were demoniacal in the presence of Vespasian, and his sons, and his captains, and the whole multitude of his soldiers. The manner of the cure was this:—He put a ring that had a root of one of those sorts mentioned by Solomon to the nostrils of the demoniac, after which he drew out the demon through his nostrils; and when the man fell down immediately, he adjured him to return into him no more, making still mention of Solomon, and reciting the incantations which he composed. And when Eleazar would persuade and demonstrate to the spectators that he had such a power, he set a little way off a cup or basin full of water, and commanded the demon as he went out of the man to overturn it, and thereby to let the spectators know that he had left the man.'

[1]Bultmann himself observes how rarely such details appear in the Gospel stories (*G.S.T.* 237; cf. Fascher, *F.M.* 128).

i

We need not doubt the word of Josephus; we may even see in such stories an illustration of the word of Jesus: 'If I by Beelzebub cast out devils, by whom do your sons cast them out?' (Lk. xi. 19); but any one who does not see the differences, as well as the similarities, between this story and the exorcisms of Jesus must surely be wanting in critical discernment. Not only this: we must also ask why such stories as these do *not* appear in the Gospels, if Bultmann is right. We ask this question, on reading his pages, but we receive no answer, for the one wonder Bultmann does not explain is the delicacy and tact of the creative community.

Much the same is true of the nature-miracles. The best parallel to the Stilling of the Storm (Mk. iv. 35-41) is the story of a Jewish child who takes a voyage in a heathen ship. During a storm all call in vain upon their gods, but when the boy prays the storm ceases and the heathen pay respect to his God (quoted by Bultmann, *G.S.T.* 249). Bultmann admits the connexion with Jonah i., but holds that the Markan story represents the intermediate stage between the two narratives. 'That here a strange wonder-story is carried over to Jesus', he says, 'appears to me not doubtful' (*G.S.T.* 250). He also abundantly illustrates from the folktales of many peoples stories of miraculous feeding, of walking on water, and of the changing of water into wine. Such stories show how accounts of miracles gather round the names of great men, and so raise the question whether this has happened in the case of Jesus. But, apart from the evidence of man's love for the miraculous, the main conclusion to be drawn from the parallels is the restraint and beauty of the Synoptic narratives. Along this line we reach no solution, but rather an enhancement of the problem.

It is surprising that investigators who compass sea and land to find parallels do not give more attention to those which stand at their door in the stories of the Acts. A story like the Lame Man at the Gate Beautiful (iii. 1-10) has the perfect three-fold form of the Miracle-Story, and although its presentation owes something to the artistry of Luke, it clearly presupposes a popular story like the longer narratives in Mark. If only it occurred in the *Antiquities*, it is safe to say that it would be seized upon with joy by the learned collectors. But it is no less a parallel story because it appears in the Acts; it reveals the popular form, and by its inherent reasonableness contributes to the solution of the problems of the Gospel stories of healing. Other parallel stories in the Acts, like that of the Raising of Aeneas (ix. 32-5), also illustrate the popular form, but so far from helping us in studying the Gospel problems they raise the difficulties in a more acute form. Only too painfully they remind us of the limitations which encompass the investigation of parallels.

III

We next ask why the Miracle-Stories were told. What object were they intended to serve?

Bultmann's view is that they were narrated as proofs of the Messianic power and divine might of Jesus (*G.S.T.* 234). He argues that they are unmotived;

they are not wrought out of pity, or to awaken faith;
they are acts which are detached from the individual will
of Jesus, and function automatically.   All the light falls
on Jesus.   Nothing is told of the inner disposition of
the sufferers or of their joy when healed.   Their faith is
not a believing relationship to the preaching or personality of Jesus; it is rather *Wunderglaube*, the trust which
is due to the miracle-worker.

This view is open to serious criticism.   The healings
are far from being involuntary outbreakings of the
divine nature of Jesus.   That they are intended is seen,
for example, by His words to the leper: 'I will; be thou
made clean'.   The one story which might lead us to
think otherwise is that of the Woman with the Issue, but
here the statement that Jesus perceived that power had
gone out from Him is the Evangelist's comment, and it
is made in this story alone.   It is quite true that we
learn nothing about the inner disposition of the sufferers, but this, Fascher claims, is characteristic of popular
narratives.   When, for example, David's child was
sick, we learn nothing of his inner feelings except
from the statement that he fasted and lay all night
upon the earth (II Sam. xii. 16; cf. Fascher, *F.M.*
122).   Further, the claim that the faith of those who
are healed is mere *Wunderglaube* will not bear examination.   The leper says: 'If thou wilt, thou canst
make me clean', and thereby proclaims his faith in
Jesus.   The distracted father of the epileptic lad
cries: 'I believe; help thou mine unbelief', and of the
woman with the issue of blood Jesus says: 'Thy faith
hath made thee whole'.   Of course, faith is not always

mentioned in these stories, but it is presupposed as
the suppliant's attitude. 'Jesus', Fascher finely says,
'does not heal "to awaken faith", because He assumes
it' (*F.M.* 125).

These arguments cut away the ground from the plea
that Miracle-Stories were told as proofs of the divinity
and Messiahship of Jesus. We need not suppose that
this motive never entered into the formative process; indeed, in a late story like that of the Marriage Feast at
Cana, it is plainly present (Jn. ii. 11); but it is not operative as the main motive in the Synoptic stories. It is
in keeping with this view that the Synoptic writers do
not represent Jesus as acting for spectacular ends, to
prove His claims, or to demonstrate His heavenly
origin. The earliest tradition is not influenced by this
motive and does not ascribe it to Jesus Himself; far from
this, it preserves His own word to His generation:
'There shall no sign be given to it but the sign of Jonah'
(Lk. xi. 29 = Mt. xii. 39). In these circumstances, we
must infer that the Miracle-Stories were told because
they illustrated the power and beneficent activity of
Jesus; and this view is supported by Acts x. 38 where
Jesus is described in the earliest preaching as one 'who
went about doing good, and healing all that were
oppressed of the devil'. In other words, the miracles
are primarily works of compassion and of power. No
doubt the idea that the power revealed is Messianic
would come in course of time to be stressed, as we see
in the Fourth Gospel (x. 25, 37f., xiv. 11); but the
Synoptic tradition antedates this stage, and even in
the Fourth Gospel the suggestion is that the 'witness'

is the result of the 'works' rather than their controlling purpose.[1]

The importance of the point under discussion is clear. If the Miracle-Stories were told as proofs of the Messiah-ship and divine might of Jesus this part of the tradition is seriously compromised; if this is not their character, the value of the stories is much greater, and the historical problem is before us in its fullest intensity.

IV

In respect of the historical problem Easton is not wholly right in the opinion that the value of Form-Criticism is 'practically negligible'[2]; for we have seen that the Miracle-Story is a distinctive narrative form, and that some of the stories stand near the records of eyewitnesses. Further, the study of parallels has shown the superiority of the Gospel stories and the distinctive place they give to faith. These are not small gains, and, so far as they go, they increase the historical value of the stories. But I should agree that in the end the study of forms brings us only to the threshold of the historical problem. This problem does not admit of any solution which can be called scientific, for our decision includes a personal element which cannot be removed; it depends on our world-view, our estimate of the Person of Christ, and our use of the principles of Historical Criticism.

[1] It is a secondary ground of appeal when the Johannine Christ says: 'Or else believe me for the very work's sake' (xiv. 11).

[2] Cf. G.G. 136. Easton is speaking of the healing-miracles. Fascher contends that the historical problem is always decided 'according to each man's world-view'. 'Therefore', he says, 'here in the last resort no methods can help, not even the form-historical (method)', F.M. 130.

It is far too late to-day to dismiss the question by say-ing that 'miracles are impossible'; that stage of the dis-cussion is definitely past.   Science takes a much humb-ler and truer view of natural law than was characteristic of former times; we now know that the 'laws of Nature' are convenient summaries of existing knowledge. Nature is not a 'closed system', and miracles are not 'intru-sions' into an 'established order.'   In the last fifty years we have been staggered too often by discoveries which at one time were pronounced impossible.   We have lived to hear of the breaking up of the atom, and to find scien-tists themselves speaking of the universe as 'more like a great thought than like a great machine'.[1]   This change of view does not, of course, accredit the miraculous; but it does mean that, given the right conditions, miracles are not impossible; no scientific or philosophic dogma stands in the way.

The importance of a true estimate of the Person of Christ cannot be over-emphasized.   If He was only a prophet the question of miracles is not worth discussing. We should certainly be ready to accept many of the healing miracles, for they are paralleled in contempor-ary stories and in the achievements of modern psycho-therapy[2]; but we should hardly consider them as more than cases of healing by 'suggestion'.   As for nature-miracles, we should at once explain them as legends, and look for natural events which have been given a miracu-lous interpretation.   But if Jesus is divine, as I believe He is; if, that is to say, the divine was revealed in His

---

[1]Sir James Jeans, *The Mysterious Universe*, 1930, p. 148.
[2]Cf. E. R. Micklem, *Miracles and the New Psychology*, 1922.

humanity in a way to which history offers no parallel; the position is profoundly altered. In this case we are still more ready to accept the healing-miracles, and to recognize that they are more than cures by 'suggestion'.[1] The stories of raising from the dead would also be easier of acceptance, for there is no reason why One such as He should not be able to recall the spirit of man from the very gates of death.

But what must be said of the nature-miracles? Here I doubt if the realities of the question have been fully faced; for these miracles are not accredited merely by the recognition that Christ was divine. The best Christian thinking has always repudiated the idea that Jesus was a demi-god in human form; it has recognized, and, with the New Testament before it, it was bound to recognize that the Incarnation imposed limitations both of knowledge and of power. How far do these limitations extend? Did they permit the power to still a storm, to multiply loaves and fishes, and to walk upon the surface of a lake? If we are honest with ourselves we have to say that we do not know; and this admission means that the full recognition of the divinity of Christ does not settle the problem of the nature-miracles. To deny that they happened is not to deny that 'the Word became flesh and dwelt among us'; it might even be consistent with a fuller appreciation of the wonder of the Incarnation.

But in arguing so we are dealing with possibilities; and it is just as much open to any one to say that the

---

[1] Micklem urges 'that it was not His practice merely to "suggest away" symptoms, but that He restored the whole personality of the sufferer, placing him in a new and right relation to life as a whole', p. 132.

nature-miracles stand *within* the limitations imposed by the Incarnation. This, one must feel, is a very difficult conception. It is true that the power to perform mighty acts does not in itself withdraw the worker from the category of humanity. We ourselves daily perform acts and use processes which fifty years ago would have been thought miraculous; we fly, we talk with people thousands of miles away, and receive messages by wireless; and, in so doing, we are not one whit less human; we love, hate, and feel, just as our fathers did. But this does not settle the question. In exercising these powers we are not less human because they have become part of the life of society, and because we are obedient to laws discovered with labour and made known to us by others. On the other hand, if Jesus multiplied loaves, He shared His power with no one; His knowledge was not won or imparted, but was born of faith in His Father. If such was His humanity, Jesus must have known a loneliness and a pain of spirit beyond anything that Christian thought has realized; for there would be many occasions when the question of the exercise of His power arose, not for self-regarding ends, or for the furtherance of His Mission—that victory was won in the wilderness—but to relieve the sufferings of men, and to make known the powers of faith. Such a conception of His humanity is possible, but no one will deny its difficulty.

But besides philosophy and theology, historical criticism must share in the inquiry. No words of Jesus forbid, or permit, us to believe that He worked miracles on Nature. His words in the Beelzebub story (Lk. xi.

19f.), and His Message to the Baptist (Lk. vii. 22f.), show that He wrought 'mighty works'; but these are works of healing and are not in dispute. Further, the words, 'There shall no sign be given unto this generation' (Mk. viii. 12), do not mean, as they have so often been said to mean, that He refused to work miracles, but only that He refused to work them as credentials to His claims.

The words of Jesus, then, do not decide the issue; we are driven, therefore, to the Synoptic narratives themselves[1]. These are few in number, and even so, are justly reduced by legitimate criticism. Few serious students will treat the Matthaean story of the Earthquake and Resurrection of the Saints (xxvii. 51*b*-3) as anything more than a late legend, and the Coin in the Fish's Mouth (Mt. xvii. 24-7), I have contended, is not a Miracle-Story at all. Many investigators also think that the so-called Miraculous Draught of Fishes (Lk. v. 1-11) does not necessarily involve a miracle, and more explain the Cursing of the Fig Tree (Mk. xi. 12-4) as a transformed parable. Thus, the problem converges on three stories: the Stilling of the Storm, the Feeding of

[1]The two stories peculiar to the Fourth Gospel do not help us in the least. We cannot recover the foundation of the story of Lazarus; for, as we have it now, the story is the result of prolonged meditation by the Evangelist, and is subservient in his hands to the desire to present Jesus as 'the resurrection and the life'. Even less helpful is the story of the Changing of Water into Wine. The narrative cannot be accepted as it stands. The occasion is too trivial; Mary's knowledge of her Son's powers is inexplicable; the amount of wine, 120 gallons, is excessive; and the distant words of Jesus, 'Woman, what have I to do with thee?' have never been adequately explained. These objections are overwhelming. The Evangelist interprets the story as a miracle, but we can only suppose that it has grown out of a natural event or an allegory.

the Five Thousand, and the Walking on the Water
(Mk. iv. 35-41; vi. 34-44; 45-52).

The question arises whether these stories are not
accounts of natural events which have been given a
miraculous interpretation. This was the view of the
older Liberal School, but it is now rejected by the
Form-Critics who explain them as legends derived from
folk-tales or shaped by popular conceptions. Easton, I
think, is right in preferring the methods of the older
Liberalism (*G.G.* 145ff.); but were the Liberals right?
No one who rationalizes the accounts of any of the
miracles can exclude this possibility in the three stories
under review. Indeed, the inquiry is demanded by the
attitude commonly taken to the story of the Gerasene
Demoniac. How easily we accept explanations which
relieve us of the need to think that Jesus 'pressed the
swine into the service of His humane endeavour'! No;
we say, the swine stampeded, frightened by the par-
oxysm of the demoniac. But if we say this, how can
we foreclose a like rationalism in the case of the nature-
miracles? And the 'explanations' are extraordinarily
easy. We have only to say that Jesus addressed the
disciples, not the winds and waves, with the words,
'Peace, be still'; that He distributed minute pieces of
bread after a sacramental custom; that He walked in the
surf of the lake, and was thought to tread the waves; and
the nature-miracles are gone. The ease of this critical
operation is not necessarily its recommendation; but it is
made distinctly easier of acceptance by the fact that in
the Markan story the miraculous feeding makes no impression on the five thousand, and that none of these

miracles is elsewhere echoed in the Synoptic tradition except in the discourse on the Leaven of the Pharisees (Mk. viii. 14-21) which has distinct difficulties of its own.

Important, however, as the critical aspects are, the problem of the nature-miracles is not solved on this side, except for those who think that Jesus was no more than a prophet; and for them the decision is easy. Those of us who believe that He was divine must also take the doctrinal considerations into account as well. Either we must reject the nature-miracles, and hold that the humanity of Jesus did not include the power to control Nature, or we must accept the stories and choose that more difficult conception of His humanity which I have already indicated. This is a very razor edge of decision. I do not think we are guilty of intellectual vacillation if we hesitate between these alternatives, now inclining to the one, now to the other. Those of us who think that the incidents were natural events ought to keep an open mind, since we may have misread the limitations of the Incarnation; and, on the other hand, those who accept the stories should ask if they do not rob the Incarnation of its grace and infinite condescension. In these matters we face unsolved problems, and each man must follow the light which he has.

No more, then, than any other kind of Criticism does Form-Criticism enable us to solve the vexed problem of the Gospel miracles; none the less, it has a real contribution to make. It enables us to affirm that the Miracle-Story is a definite form of oral tradition closely related to the life and faith of the earliest Christianity. It permits us to distinguish between stories in free circulation and stories which stand nearer primitive accounts. By comparing like stories in Jewish and Hellenistic tradition it reveals the worth of the Gospel stories, and gives us no reason to think that they have been formed by a process of borrowing. It supplies no basis for the inference that doctrinal interests were responsible for their formation, or indeed that they arose out of any other motive than the desire to illustrate the power and compassion of Jesus. If at this point the investigator of forms is compelled to hand on the problem to the historical critic, to make such a decision as he can, he is at least able to claim that he has placed the critic in the best position possible from which to approach the Gospel narratives. The rest depends on our use of Historical Criticism, our world-view, and our estimate of Jesus.

THE STORIES ABOUT JESUS

IN my second lecture I pointed out that the Stories about Jesus have no common structural form, and that the term 'Legend' prejudges their historical value, since, in common usage, the name expresses a historical judgment. If this is so, it is not possible to classify them on formal principles, and we must describe them as the 'Narrative-tradition' or as 'Stories about Jesus'.

This opinion does not mean that there is nothing to be learnt about these stories from the formal standpoint; it means that we cannot reduce them to a standard form, with a peculiar history of its own, related to special interests and answering a common need. We have to take each story by itself, or examine them in groups which are not always mutually exclusive. Two features at least these stories share with those already discussed: most of them are isolated or self-contained stories, and all are intimately connected with the life and the interests of primitive Christianity.

I

The first thing that strikes the student of the Narrative-tradition is its scanty character. If we remove from Mark all Pronouncement- and Miracle-Stories, all say-

ings-groups, isolated sayings, parables, and editorial
passages, only eighteen stories are left outside the Passion-narrative.   In Matthew in the same circumstances
only two narratives and the Birth Stories remain, apart
from additions to Markan stories and the narratives from
Q.   Luke supplies eleven stories from his special tradition in addition to his Birth Stories, and the Fourth
Evangelist about fourteen.   In other words, besides the
accounts of the Birth, Death, and Resurrection of Jesus,
there are approximately fifty Stories about Jesus in all
the Gospels.   Some of these, as for example in the
Fourth Gospel, are of literary rather than popular origin,
and of the popular stories most are self-contained narratives.   These facts raise an interesting question which
has been much debated in recent years: Had the first
Christians a biographical interest?

So far as the Evangelists are concerned, somewhat
different answers must be given.   None of them aims
at producing a biography in the modern sense of the
term, although all wish to tell the Story of Jesus.   In
the Fourth Gospel the dominant aims are religious and
doctrinal, but the material is presented in a historical
framework.   In Mark there is present a desire to sketch
in outline the course of the Ministry of Jesus, and the
same outline is followed in Matthew, although here it is
subordinated to didactic and ecclesiastical interests.   In
Luke the sixfold date of iii. 1f., and the terms of the Preface (i. 1-4) indicate an intention to tell the Story in
orderly succession, although we cannot assume that
chronological succession is meant, or still less is achieved.   The tentative nature of the efforts of Mark and

Luke is eloquent of the conditions as they existed in the earlier oral period. The Evangelists could not succeed because for a generation at least a Christianity had existed which was destitute of the biographical interest: no one thought of recording the life of Christ.

The want of this interest is not disproved by the early existence of connected Passion Stories, for these, as we have seen, arose out of practical needs; it is confirmed by the Birth Stories, for these are late literary compilations; it is proved by the fact that the Stories about Jesus are isolated stories; we might call them 'anecdotes' if the associations of the word were better. Of course, if by a 'biographical interest' we mean a wish to tell stories from the life of Jesus, the first Christians had such an interest; but if we mean the desire to trace the course of a man's life, to show how one thing led to another, to depict the development of his personality, to make him real to the imagination and the understanding, the first Christians had no such interest. That is why it is only approximately that we can infer the age of Jesus, the year He began His work, and the duration of His Ministry. We know nothing of His personal appearance. Passing references to His habit of looking at men, to His sighs, His anger, His withdrawals for prayer, are examples of the few personal details which are recorded. By far the greater part of His life is unknown. The Markan Gospel enables us to detect turning-points in His Mission, but even this Gospel is full of gaps which could not be filled at the time when Mark wrote.

The results of this want of a literary interest on the part of primitive Christianity are not an unmixed evil.

Our curiosity is left unsatisfied, and many things per-
plex us; but at any rate we are spared the distortions
which early biographies would have entailed. Nothing
is so revealing as a biography—about the author! But
we can dispense with fuller knowledge about the Evangelists because we have been spared the veil which well-
intentioned biographers would have cast over the face
of Jesus. Because the Gospels are not biographies,
we know Him better.

Several reasons can be suggested for the want of a biographical interest. First, the early Christians were men
of humble origin and attainments; they were not a literary people, and so did not face the problems which confront the chronicler. Further, their eyes were on the
New Heaven and the New Earth which they believed
Christ would soon bring. They did not know that
nineteen centuries later we should still lack the consum-
mation: nothing would have astonished them more.
Their hopes were on the future; what need was there to
record the past? Again, the formation of Jesus-tradi-
tion was largely a communal process. Stories had sur-
vival-value, not so much because they had interest for
the individual, but because they ministered to the needs
of Christians who met together in religious fellowship.
There must have been many stories of invaluable interest to the modern man which had no chance of survival,
because they knocked in vain at the doors of communal
faith. They were not deliberately ignored; they were
not appreciated because they did not minister to univer-
sal needs. The tradition welcomed was that which
ministered to faith and justified existing practices; which

K

answered questions and met the objections of hostile critics; which illuminated relationships between individuals in the community and between the community and the outside world.   What was wanted was a standard of life, and this was found in the words and deeds of Jesus; the stories cherished were those which set the standard. Wherever this principle is transcended, we have either legends, or stories which survived because the narrators stood in a favoured relationship to 'eyewitnesses and ministers of the word'.

II

I will first call your attention to the eighteen Stories about Jesus in Mark.   These narratives cannot be further classified into sharply defined forms; none the less formal distinctions can be made among them which are worth noting.

1. First of all there are a few stories which appear to be literary compositions; they have been put together by the Evangelist from fragments of existing tradition. The story of the Preaching of the Baptist is of this character (i. 5-8).   The story is told not as an eyewitness would have told it, but rather from the standpoint of Mark's day.   The Evangelist describes the great impression John's preaching produced, and mentions his food and clothing, but he gives no account of the Baptist's apocalyptic message as Q does.   Mark is interested in one point only—John's prophecy of the Coming One, and, even so, the prophecy of a baptism by fire is softened into that of a baptism by the Spirit.   This happens because Mark is selecting elements from tradi-

tion which will serve best to introduce his account of the Story of Jesus. In like manner the two following stories, the Baptism (i. 9-11), and the Temptation (i. 12f.), are also summaries, though Mark correctly preserves the tradition that in the Baptism Jesus experienced a vision which led to the Temptation. The only other story of the kind is the Leaven of the Pharisees (viii. 14-21). Only the bold will think that they understand this story. As it stands it appears to be influenced by the view that the two Feeding stories describe separate miraculous events, and this opinion, already current in Mark's day, has left its imprint on the recorded words of Jesus. The merit of the story is that it preserves the idea of something spiritual and mysterious in the incident in the wilderness. Mark is using material given to him by the tradition, which apparently he does not fully understand himself. Such, at least, is the impression which the narrative leaves on the modern mind, and his procedure is far removed from that of the inventor of pious legends.

2. Distinct from these stories are others of a more popular kind, which Mark reproduces very much as he receives them. Such a story, for example, is that of Herod and Jesus (vi. 14-6); it is brief and appears to be adapted to the story of the Death of John which follows, and which A. E. J. Rawlinson well describes as an account of 'what was being darkly whispered in the bazaars or market-places of Palestine at the time' (*St. Mark*, p. 82). Herod may have said: 'John, whom I beheaded, he is risen', but Luke's version: 'John I beheaded: but who is this?' sounds more convincing.

Another story of the kind is that of the Child in the Midst
(ix. 33-7) which may at one time have been a Pronouncement-Story, like that of the Blessing of the Children (x.
13-6), but ending with a different saying. On the bor-
der-line between this group and the next is the story of
the Syro-Phoenician Woman (vii. 24-30), which also
may have a similar history (cf. p. 76). Interest in the
Gentile Mission no doubt commended the story to Mark
and his Roman readers, despite the words : 'Let the children first be filled'; but the witty answer of the woman:
'Yea, Lord: even the dogs under the table eat of the children's crumbs', is a transcript from life.

3. The eleven stories that remain, like some of the
Miracle-Stories, are personal as well as popular stories;
they are in no sense 'legends', and, since they are so well
preserved a generation after the Ministry of Jesus, they
must have come to Mark along personal channels. The
Call of the First Disciples (i. 16-20) and the Call of Levi
(ii. 14) have the note of historical realism. It has often
been remarked that the former story reads like a recast
in the third person of the incident as it appeared to the
fishers on the lake. Bultmann's alternative explanation (*G.S.T.* 27, 67) that the story was spun out of the
saying about 'fishers of men' is quite unsatisfactory, it is
much more likely that the metaphor was suggested by
the circumstances. The reference also to the 'hired
servants' who remained with Zebedee in the boat is far
better explained as a personal reminiscence than as an
imaginative touch supplied by Mark.

The story of the Departure into a Desert Place (i.
35-9) is the last of the closely articulated series of four

to which I referred in the second lecture (p. 39). In view of the character of these Capernaum stories, and the fact that Peter is specially mentioned in two of them, it is best to suppose that the series comes from Peter. The story of the Departure in particular suggests this. Mark knows that Jesus rose early while it was yet night, and uses a very descriptive word (κατεδίωξεν, 'tracked down') to describe Peter's pursuit of Jesus, which ends with the cry: 'All are seeking thee'. What genius would have invented the discouraging reply, so true to the mind of Jesus: 'Let us go elsewhere into the next towns, that I may preach there also; for to this end came I forth'? Even a story like the Appointment of the Twelve (iii. 13-9), which involves the mention of a list of names, has the same note of historical realism. Only good tradition can account for the explanation that Jesus appointed Twelve 'that they might be with him, and that he might send them forth to preach, and to have authority to cast out devils'.

Peter is not mentioned in the Visit to Nazareth (vi. 1-6a), but the story is of the same character as those already mentioned. Not to dwell on the perfectly natural question of the Nazarenes, and the reference to the brothers and sisters of Jesus, we are beyond the range of invention in the statements that Jesus 'could there do no mighty work', and that 'he marvelled because of their unbelief'.

Peter's Confession (viii. 27-30) and the three Prophecies of the Passion (viii. 31-3; ix. 30-2; x. 32-4) may be taken together. The historical character of the Confession is guaranteed by the words: 'Get thee behind me,

Satan: for thou mindest not the things of God, but the things of men'.   The prophecies are widely regarded as 'Christian formations', because of the express reference to the Resurrection 'after three days', and because, if Jesus spoke these words, the attitude of the disciples and of the women after the Crucifixion seems inexplicable (cf. Schmidt, *R.G.J.* 218).   But this view is not necessary, especially if it is allowed that the terms of the original forecasts have been sharpened in the light of subsequent events.   In consequence of their presuppositions, it is not incredible if the disciples did not understand the prophecies at the time; Peter's bold rebuke shows what their attitude must have been.   Moreover, the third prophecy is preceded by one of the most vivid passages in Mark: 'And Jesus was going before them: and they were amazed; and they that followed were afraid' (x. 32).   These arguments ought not to suffer prejudice because they are on the side of orthodoxy; they are altogether superior to those by which the prophecies are rejected.

The Transfiguration 'after six days' (ix. 2-10) is a credible, though mysterious vision-experience, as Ed. Meyer maintains (*U.A.*, i. 152-7), and is better accounted for in this way than as a Resurrection Appearance which has been antedated and read back into the life of Jesus (Bultmann, *G.S.T.* 278-81).   As in other stories where Peter is mentioned, there is vividness of description in the phrase: 'so as no fuller on earth can whiten them', and a characteristic note in the cry: 'Let us make three tabernacles'.   The two remaining stories of this class are the Entry into Jerusalem and the Cleansing of the

Temple. The former (xi. 1-11) is one of the most detailed of the Markan stories. In the words: 'and
straightway he will send him back hither', the idea of an
arrangement previously made by Jesus is suggested
which apparently both Matthew and Luke have missed.
No legend would have broken off the account with the
anticlimax: 'and when he had looked round about upon
all things, it being now eventide, he went out unto Bethany with the twelve', and it is only as a reminiscence that
this statement is natural. The Cleansing (xi. 15-8) also
leaves a good impression of historical worth which is
justly appraised only when the brevity of the story is
noted.

The observations I made regarding several of the
Miracle-Stories apply also to some of the narratives just
considered, although perhaps not to the same degree;
they are too detailed to be treated as stories told and retold by a series of nameless narrators.[1] Although not
the records of an eyewitness, they stand near such testimony. Another point to be noticed is that nearly all
the eleven stories have to do with turning-points in the
Story of Jesus. If the editorial passages are the cement
of the loosely-constructed Markan Gospel, these stories
are its foundation stones. This association of inward
and outward circumstances cannot be accidental, and
seems to me to go far to confirm the opinion I expressed
in the second lecture (cf. p. 42f.) regarding Mark's de-
pendence on Peter's preaching. Two years ago I expressed agreement with the opinion that, if we had
not the Papias tradition, we should require to assume

[1]Cf. F. C. Burkitt, *Church and Gnosis*, 1932, p. 143.

something like it (*G.* 70). A renewed study of Mark from the standpoint of Form-Criticism has served to deepen this conviction.

III

When from the Markan Stories about Jesus we pass to those in Matthew we enter another realm. The narratives are few in number and are like the Matthaean additions to Mark's Passion Story; they assume existing tradition and seek to answer the questions it raises. This is so, for example, in the addition to the Baptism story (iii. 14f.):

'But John would have hindered him, saying, "I have need to be baptized of thee, and comest thou to me?" But Jesus answering said unto him, "Suffer it now; for thus it becometh us to fulfil all righteousness". Then he suffered him.'

This story replies to the difficulties of those who thought it strange that Jesus should have been baptized by John. The addition to the Miracle-Story of the Walking on the Water (xiv. 28-33) is true to the character of Peter, but it is wanting in vivid detail, and ends conventionally with the words: 'And they that were in the boat worshipped him, saying, "Of a truth thou art the Son of God".' The Matthaean Birth-Stories answer problems raised by the Virgin Birth. The story of the Birth of Jesus (i. 18-25) is really an account of how Joseph's fears were allayed. The stories of the Wise Men (ii. 1-12) and the Departure to and Return from Egypt (ii. 13-23) suggest the homage of the Gentile world, and trace parallels between the experience of Moses and that of Jesus. What basis in fact these stories have, it is impossible now to say,[1] but the conclusion is irresistible that here, in contrast with both Mark and Luke, apologetic and doctrinal interests are uppermost.

IV

We will next consider the eleven stories which precede the Lukan Passion-narrative. These are: the Sermon at Nazareth, the Call of the Disciples, the Woman in the City, the Samaritan Village, the Mission and Return of the Seventy, Martha and Mary, Jesus and Herod, the Ten Lepers, Zacchaeus, the Rejoicing of the Disciples, and the Weeping over Jerusalem.[2] I have suggested that three of these—the Woman in the City, the Samaritan Village, and the Ten Lepers—may at one time have been Pronouncement-Stories, but in all the eleven stories as we have them now the narrative element predominates.

In some respects these Lukan stories provide a better illustration of the narrative tradition of an early Palestinian community than that furnished by the Markan stories, for through his association with Peter, Mark enjoyed advantages which were not shared by Luke.[3] The characteristics of the Lukan tradition are those we should naturally expect in a community outside Jerusalem, such as that of Caesarea.

[1] Cf. G. H. Box, *The Virgin Birth of Jesus*, 22.

[2] Lk. iv. 16-30; v. 1-11; vii. 36-50; ix. 52b-6; x. 1, 17-20, 38-42; xiii. 31-3; xvii. 11-9; xix. 1-10, 39-40, 41-4.

[3] The difference appears to me to be accounted for by the difference in the intermediaries rather than by the time-interval.

1. In the first place, there is a tendency for details to pass over from one story to another. The process is not deliberate; it happens as stories are passed from hand to hand, helped by the tendency to bring like to like. The story of the Woman in the City (vii. 36-50) supplies an illustration. This incident, I think, is different from that of the Anointing related in Mk. xiv. 3-9. The one happens at an unnamed place in the house of a Pharisee, the other at Bethany in the house of a former leper. In the Lukan story the woman is a 'sinner', in Mark there is no reason to suppose this. The one woman anoints the feet of Jesus, wetting them with her tears, the other anoints His head. In the one story the deed is a sign of penitence, in the other it is an act of love which Jesus applies to His burial. So far the stories are different, and yet they leave on the mind an inescapable sense of similarity. In each case the host is called Simon; both incidents happen while Jesus sits at meat, and in each story an alabaster cruse of ointment is brought. Further, there are striking parallels, along with differences, between the Johannine account of the Anointing (xii. 1-7) and details in Mark and Luke. In the Johannine story the woman is identified with Mary the sister of Martha and Lazarus. As in Luke, the feet of Jesus are anointed and wiped with the woman's hair, but the rest of the story follows Mark.

All theories which suggest that Luke has adapted the Markan story to a new situation seem to me crude and unsatisfactory, for, from abundant examples, we know how closely he reproduces Markan stories and respects their place in the Markan outline. Why should his procedure here be so diametrically different?   It is far better, and much more probable, to presuppose a transference of details in the course of oral tradition.

I have worked out this illustration more fully than is possible in other examples.   The Lukan story of the Call of the Disciples shares details with the corresponding Markan story (i. 16-20) and others with the Johannine account of the appearance of the Risen Lord to the disciples by the Sea of Galilee (xxi. 1-14).   The Ten Lepers (Lk. xvii. 11-9) recalls the Markan story of the Cure of a Leper (i. 40-5).   A similar saying of Jesus appears in the two stories of the Bent Woman (Lk. xiii. 10-7) and the Dropsical Man (Lk. xiv. 1-6), and in the latter story and the Markan account of the Man with the Withered Hand (iii. 1-5) Jesus asks the same question. It is obviously impossible to unravel the tangled threads, nor can we safely assume that in every case they belong to one story alone; but, since the same problem meets us so often in the Lukan stories, we are right in concluding that this cycle of tradition, more than others, is marked by a transference of details.

2. A second feature of the Lukan stories is their typical aspect: a single story focusses many incidents of the same kind.   By this I do not mean that the stories are ideal constructions, but that they are representative. This is true, for example, of the Sermon at Nazareth (iv. 16-30) which is meant to supply a typical picture of the synagogue activity of Jesus and of its fortunes; it is true also of healing miracles like the Ten Lepers, of social experiences like those indicated in the story of Martha and Mary (x. 38-42), of redemptive works like that

described in the story of Zacchaeus (xix. 1-10). When we see Jesus in the house of Martha, we see Him often in fellowship with His friends. When we enter with Him into the house of Zacchaeus, we follow Him often in pursuit of men neglected and despised by the religious leaders of His day. When we watch Him by the bier at the gate of Nain (vii. 11-7), we see His sympathy with all who are overwhelmed by bereavement and loss. This fact has its bearings on the limitations of the Lukan narrative-tradition. The stories are few, but they are typical; and it was because they were typical that they were cherished by the Caesarean community.[1] In a sense there was no need for more, since all was here.

3. A third characteristic of the Lukan stories is their symbolic aspect: they suggest ideas precious to the community and to Luke himself. Can we read the story of the Synagogue at Nazareth without thinking of the rejection of the Gospel by the Jews? Does not the command in the Call of the Disciples, 'Put out into the deep, and let down your nets for a draught', followed by the reference to a catch so great that 'their nets were breaking', point to the Gentile Mission? Is not the same thought manifest in the story of the Mission and Return of the Seventy, a number which in Gen. x. represents the nations of the world? Is not universalism symbolized in the Samaritan stories, and love for the redemptive work of Jesus reflected in the stories of Zacchaeus and the Penitent Thief? Any hesitation we feel regarding this aspect of the Lukan stories is largely due to the

[1]Cf. also the Acts where Luke summarizes the record by relating a few stories, or even one.

fear that, in admitting its presence, we dislodge their roots in the soil of history. The best way to meet this fear is to study the writings of those who perform the uprooting operation to their own satisfaction, as is done, for example, in Loisy's *L'Évangile selon Luc* (1924). According to Loisy, the Third Gospel is not a historical work, but a cult-legend. The story of the Widow's Son prefigures the salvation of Israel, while that of the Centurion's Servant prefigures the salvation of Gentiles. Martha and Mary represent two sections of the primitive Church, the Judaeo-Christian and the Hellenistic-Christian parties. The parable of the Good Samaritan illustrates the superiority of the Christian over the Jew in the fulfilling of the law. Now this is criticism run to seed; it exploits the symbolism of the stories in the interests of a historical theory.[1] It is one thing to say that symbolism shines through a story of fact, quite another thing to say symbolism is clothing itself with the garb of reality. Both types of narratives are found in literature, but the second is entirely a product of the imagination. If the Lukan stories were of this kind they would be richer and more varied. How many ideas belonging to later Church history and organization might so easily have been embodied in 'sacred legends'! This mode of interpretation, moreover, compels us to exaggerate the art of the stories: we have to find symbolism in simple and innocent statements, flights of fancy in the work of one who claims to give plain facts about things in which his readers have been instructed

---

[1] I have discussed these points in an article in the *Hibbert Journal* (xxiv. 563-72) on 'The Alleged Neglect of M. Alfred Loisy'.

(Lk. i. 1-4). The symbolism, we may be sure, is not a product of the imagination; it lies within the facts that are told.

These characteristics have an obvious bearing on the historical value of the Lukan tradition. In *Behind the Third Gospel* I drew attention to the presence in the stories of 'the curious combination of simplicity and directness with a certain vagueness of outline' (p. 251). I feel sure that this description fits the case, and that the explanation is the same as in some of the Miracle-Stories. The stories have been shortened and rounded in the course of oral transmission; they have passed from hand to hand, and have been made the subject of comment and reflection, with the result that many a vivid detail has fallen by the way while the historical core remains.[1]

A general statement of this kind will not cover the whole of the tradition. It accounts excellently for stories like the Call of the Disciples, the Samaritan Village, the Ten Lepers, and Zacchaeus. On the other hand a story like that of Herod and Jesus (xiii. 31-3) has more of the freshness of originality, and perhaps the same is true of the story of Martha and Mary. As distinct from these stories, those of the Sermon at Nazareth and the Woman in the City show more signs of Luke's literary art. As in the story of the Two going to Emmaus, and in some of the Illustrative-Stories, his brush moves more freely on the canvas, and he gives his powers the freedom of a great artist. It is worth considering whether, in thus enriching the tradition, Luke

[1]See Appendix B.

has not actually come nearer to the pictorial art of Jesus Himself.   The real question is not whether the Lukan tradition is a bare transcript from fact, but whether it gives a true portraiture of the events described.   Judged by this test, it stands well.   What does it matter, except for the pedant, if some of the pictures are composite, if in the Mission of the Seventy or the Ten Lepers, round numbers are used, or even if the beliefs of the community shine through the narratives?   In spite of these features the stories give a real and valuable contribution to our knowledge of Jesus.

v

I now turn to the Lukan Birth Stories.   Nowhere is the variety of the Narrative-tradition so apparent, for here we find, not self-contained stories, but a continuous narrative, and yet a narrative which is very different in form from the Passion Story.   The section consists of several scenes, some of which are parallel to one another, and the whole forms a kind of miniature Birth and Infancy drama.   The scenes include two Annunciation stories (i. 5-25; 26-38), followed by the Meeting of Mary and Elisabeth (i. 39-56); and two Birth stories (i. 57-8; ii. 1-7), followed in the one case by the account of John's Circumcision and the Song of Zacharias (i. 59-80), and in the other by the Visit of the Shepherds, the Circumcision of Jesus, the Presentation in the Temple, and the Greeting of Simeon and Anna (ii. 8-40); and the series closes with the story of the Visit of the Boy Jesus to Jerusalem at the age of twelve (ii. 41-52).

The section itself, and the knowledge we have already

gained of the formation of early Christian tradition, suggest that Lk. i. 5–ii. 52 is a literary composition of no mean order which ought to be treated as inspired poetry rather than as sober prose. This is indicated by the fact that a considerable part of the Birth Stories consists of songs and speeches which appear to be formed on Old Testament models, and it is confirmed by the obvious contrast between this part of the Gospel and the rest of the special Lukan tradition outside the Passion-narrative. If the Galilean material is so fragmentary, how was it that Luke was able to write a continuous account of events thirty years earlier? There is no satisfactory answer to this question except the conclusion that the Birth Stories are a literary compilation.

Is Luke, or some earlier writer on whom he depends, responsible for the compilation? Unfortunately, critical opinion is divided on this question. Some scholars believe that Luke translated an existing Hebrew or Aramaic original, basing their contention on passages in the Greek which are alleged to be mistranslations of the source. Arguments of this kind rarely lead to decisive conclusions. C. C. Torrey, for example, appeals to the phrase ἐποίησε κράτος ἐν βραχίονι αὐτοῦ (i. 51) as containing evidence of the kind, but W. F. Howard observes that, while 'the Hebraic phraseology is beyond question', there is nothing in the phrase which could not have been composed 'by one who was steeped in the diction of the Greek version of the Psalter'.[1] Far from thinking that Luke translated an Aramaic original, both

---

[1] Cf. his Appendix on Semitisms in Moulton's *Grammar of New Testament Greek*, vol. ii. (1929), 483.

J. H. Moulton and the Abbé Lagrange doubt if he knew Aramaic. Harnack has forcibly argued that no Greek source can have been used, and that Luke probably composed the section on the basis of oral tradition and with the intention of closely reproducing the language of the Septuagint. Where differences of opinion are so great, it is not possible to say more than that the balance of the argument inclines to the view that Luke himself composed the Birth Stories. All the indications are that he did so at a relatively late date. This follows at once if Proto-Luke (60-5 A.D.) began with the sixfold date of iii. 1f., the Preaching of John, the Baptism, and the Genealogy. It is also implied if the section is a literary composition. Activity of this kind is hard to understand unless it belongs to the seventies or the eighties, and on the whole it is best to date the Birth Stories during the period 75-80 A.D.

The main interest of the Birth Stories for us to-day hardly lies in minute discussions about points of detail, but in the question how we are to understand them as a whole. In this matter more confident statements are possible. The Birth Stories represent the Evangelist's attempt, with the material at his disposal, to express in a poetic and imaginative form definite convictions about the birth and divine significance of Jesus. To Luke Jesus comes along the pathway of Old Testament promise. He is God's Son, born of Mary, who fulfils in Himself ancient and existing Messianic expectations. I have elsewhere argued (*The Historical Evidence for the Virgin Birth*, 1920) that this is the original significance of the Birth Stories, and that i. 34f., which asserts the

L

Virgin Birth, was superimposed on the original narrative by Luke himself. Other views widely held are that this passage is integral to the story, or that, on the other hand, it is a non-Lukan interpolation.

The literary problem raises the whole question of the Virgin Birth. This problem occupies a curious position from the fact that few scholars seem particularly anxious to face it. The literary critics who do not reject the Virgin Birth say that it is finally a question for the theologians; and the theologians gracefully hand back the problem to the literary critics, expressing the opinion that, while congruous with the doctrine of the Incarnation, the manner of the Birth is not essential to that doctrine, and that the question remains a matter for historical inquiry.[1] The critics reply that the doctrine was not known to Mark or Paul, was replaced without necessarily being denied by the Fourth Evangelist in his doctrine of the Divine Logos, and appears only in the least valuable historical strata in Matthew and perhaps, but not certainly, in the poetic Birth narrative of Luke. The result for the instructed Christian is an atmosphere of indecision and uncertainty. The truth is, there is not, and cannot be, a completely scientific judgment on this question, if we have regard to all the facts of the case. Where the Virgin Birth is accepted, it is held mainly because it is found in Scripture and in the great Creeds of the Church. If, in these circumstances, I may venture an opinion, it is that the New Testament evidence is so scanty and so late that increased acceptance is likely to be given as time goes by to the position held by the late

[1]But see J. G. Machen, *The Virgin Birth of Christ*, 1930, pp. 380-97.

Canon Sanday who accepted the Supernatural Birth of
Jesus, but interpreted the Virgin Birth tradition symboli-
cally.

VI

I fear I can make little more than a reference to the
Stories about Jesus in the Fourth Gospel; but it is worth
while to do even this, if only to illustrate the difference
in form between the Johannine and the Synoptic stories.
Very few of the narratives in the Fourth Gospel are brief
and self-contained, and those which are of this character
—the Nobleman's Son (iv. 46-54), the Anointing (xii.
1-7), and the Entry into Jerusalem[1] (xii. 12-9)—have
parallels in the earlier Gospels.   Far from being isolated
units, many of the Johannine stories are closely associated with discourses or controversial debates, as in the
Cleansing (ii. 13-22), the Further Witness of John (iii.
22-30), the Coming of the Greeks (xii. 20-4), and the
Feet-washing (xiii. 4-10).   In longer stories like Nico-
demus (iii. 1-21), the Impotent Man at Bethesda (v.
1-16), and the Feeding of the Five Thousand (vi. 1-14),
this is still more apparent.   So marked is this feature in
the Fourth Gospel, that the absence of a discourse or a
discussion in connexion with the Changing of Water
into Wine (ii. 1-10) causes surprise.

The most notable feature of the Johannine Narrative-
tradition is the marked dramatic element in stories like
the Woman of Samaria (iv. 1-42), the Man Born Blind
(ix. 1-38), and the Raising of Lazarus (xi. 1-46).   As

---

[1] The Entry, however, is linked by the Evangelist with the story of
Lazarus (cf. xii. 17f.).

J. M. Thompson and H. Windisch have shown (*J.E.*
178ff.), these stories can easily be arranged in the form
of short dramas, or dramatic sketches, each including a
series of scenes; and, to a less degree, this is true of the
Baptist's Testimony (i. 19-39) and the Call of the First
Disciples (i. 40-51). In the Woman of Samaria the
first scene is silent: Jesus approaches the well and sits
down in weariness, while the disciples go into the city to
buy food (vv. 5, 6 and 8). In the second scene (vv. 7-
26) the interview with the woman takes place. The
third scene portrays the disciples' return; they are surprised to see Jesus talking with a woman, while the
woman herself departs leaving her waterpot at the well
(v. 27f.). Scene four (v. 29f.) is placed in the town of
Sychar: the woman summons her townsmen to come
and see Jesus. Scene five (vv. 31-8) follows in the
meantime: Jesus is asked by His disciples to eat, and
discourses on spiritual food and fields white unto har-
vest. In scene six (vv. 39-41) the Samaritans arrive and
ask Jesus to abide with them. Scene seven (v. 42), two
days later, contains the Samaritans' testimony to the
woman, and is the climax of the whole: 'Now we believe,
not because of thy speaking: for we have heard for ourselves, and know that this is indeed the Saviour of the
world'.

The art present in these stories is undeniable, and
must to a considerable extent be conscious art: but this
cannot be a complete explanation, for some of the scenes
are bare, and would probably have been more fully developed, if the artistic interest had been uppermost. I
do not think that we can adequately account for these

stories unless we have regard to the Evangelist's personality and experience. We must also appreciate the difference between the tradition as he received it, and the form it came to assume in his own mind. What the original form was we can only imagine. The Fourth Evangelist does not reproduce the tradition as a chronicler would present it, nor even as the Synoptists record it. Long before he takes up his pen to write, the Narrative-tradition has been the object of his reflection and meditation. He sees the tradition in the light of a remarkably rich Christian experience, and is one of those thinkers who delight to find deep significance in the details of a story. He is not, however, an abstract thinker, but one whose thoughts take form and colour, and are visualized and seen in dramatic form. I do not think we need to go further and suppose, with Miss Underhill and Canon Streeter (*F.G.* 390-2), that the stories had their origin in a kind of mystic vision, or are visions veridical in character. Actual events, seen or reported, seem to me to constitute a sufficient basis for the transforming process which, in any case, is the secret of the Johannine narratives. If this is their origin, it is obvious that it is quite out of place to test these stories by the kind of historical standard we apply to the Markan and the Lukan stories. In the Fourth Gospel, we are dealing with stories in which there is a clear interpretative element, and we must appreciate this fact in evaluating them. Their value does not lie in the preservation of historical detail, but in the significance which is found in, and brought out of, the original tradition. This is not something to regret, much less to apologize for; it is

of infinite value to us to-day to have included in the
variety of primitive Christian tradition one Gospel
which, more than all others, is concerned to tell us what
the historical facts mean, and this is especially the case
when that Gospel is the work of so great a spiritual
genius.

VII

A few brief comments must serve to conclude a lecture already long.   The survey I have made shows the
variety of the Stories about Jesus.   It fully confirms the
opinion that there is no one narrative-form for material
of this kind comparable to the Pronouncement-Story or
the Miracle-Story.   To say this is not to deny that the
narratives have common formal characteristics.   In almost all cases Jesus stands in the centre and usually
secondary characters are not named or described.   Con-
versations take place between two persons, or between
Jesus and a group; in a few stories only, like the Penitent Thief, are three speakers introduced.   These features suggest that practical aims rather than narrative
interests are responsible for the formation of these
stories, and that the formative process is less one of embellishment than one of shortening; secondary features
fade out and are forgotten, and the figure of Jesus comes
into stronger focus.   This is exactly what ought to be
the history of a genuine historical tradition; it is the reverse of that which is found in the apocryphal literature.
The result, then, of a study of the formal aspects of the
Stories about Jesus is to strengthen confidence in their
historical value.

The survey has shown that for the most part the stories are self-contained. This, again, is a feature of oral tradition which, as a rule, is content to record incidents rather than a sequence of events. The exceptions are the Petrine stories of Mark, the Birth Stories of Luke, and the Johannine narratives. If the study of exceptions is important, these narratives cannot be too carefully considered. In the Lukan Birth Stories and the Johannine narratives the continuity is a sign of literary art. Because this explanation will not suit the Petrine Stories, we are driven to conclude that, where continuity is present in these narratives, it is due to a personal witness received from Peter.

VIII

THE EMERGENCE OF THE GOSPELS

ONE of the tests of a historical study is the ability to tell a story of events. From the stones, glassware, pottery, and jewels which he recovers from a lost civilization, the archaeologist can recreate the past and tell us much about the lives and thoughts of people long since dead; and his power to do this is part of the justification of his work. The same is true of the historian, and in a measure it ought to be possible for the literary critic. It goes without saying that in any recreation of the past much has to be supplied by the imagination; but there is all the difference in the world between idle fancy and the historical imagination controlled by facts which have been patiently investigated. Such a story I shall now attempt to tell in respect of the Gospel tradition.

In this undertaking we are helped by the knowledge given to us by contemporary history and by the Acts and the New Testament Epistles, but our main authorities must be the Gospels themselves. And these writings ought to be able to tell us a great deal, for documents are surely more eloquent than broken pottery. If there are sermons in stones, there ought to be historical messages in stories and in sayings which can be traced behind the Gospels themselves.

It is obvious that in an undertaking of this kind detailed arguments and laboured justifications must be avoided.   For the most part the arguments have been given in the earlier lectures; what we now require to see is the resultant picture which forms within the mind if the previous arguments are valid.

I propose to trace the story through three periods, extending from 30 to 50 A.D., from 50 to 65, and from 65 to 100.   In describing the lecture by the title, 'The Emergence of the Gospels', I am thinking less of questions of authorship, date, and sources, although these points cannot be ignored, and more of the vital conditions out of which the Gospels came into being.

I

During the years which immediately followed the Resurrection, the first Christians preserved cycles of connected reminiscences associated with the various centres of the Ministry of Jesus.   This kind of recollection was in the nature of things, and is the explanation of the Passion-narratives and of those short connected cycles of Markan tradition which have to do with Capernaum (i. 21-39) and the Sea of Galilee (iv. 35-v. 43; vi. 30–viii. 26).   Naturally, this information was very much fuller than that which is accessible to us now in the Gospels; but it was not guided and sustained by a biographical interest, and accordingly it soon began to perish by an inevitable process of attrition.   Practical interests were uppermost, and thus it was that within about a decade the Gospel tradition came to be mainly a collection of isolated stories, sayings, and

sayings-groups. The most important exception to the
dissolving process continued to be the Passion Story
which existed in the form of short accounts of the Arrest, Trial, and Crucifixion of Jesus current at different
centres of primitive Christianity.

The first Passion Stories were shaped by the earliest
preaching and by repetition during the meetings of
the communities to break bread. There is no need to
distinguish sharply between the influences exerted by
preaching and by worship, much less to regard them as
alternative formative factors; each contributed to the
shaping of the Story, and one often passed into the other.
It is unlikely that the primitive record was drafted by a
central Apostolic Council, for, had it been so, the tradition would be more fixed and the existence of different
Passion Stories would be hard to explain. The principal agents who shaped the tradition were eyewitnesses
and others who had knowledge of the original facts.
Constant repetition, especially in connexion with early
celebrations of the Supper, gave relative fixity to the
Story, and yet not such a fixity as to leave no room for
additions. Early Christian leaders moved from one
community to another (cf. Acts viii. 1, 14, 26; ix. 32,
etc.), and, as a result of this, details prized in one community would find entrance into the Story of another
community. Moreover, the Passion Story as it was
told in important Churches would often replace local
versions which were felt to be less worthy, or wanting in
Apostolical authority. In this way the Markan Story
came to establish itself far and wide. In Antioch—if
this is the city in which Matthew's Gospel gained pub-

licity—no other account of the Passion can now be traced, since the Matthaean additions presuppose the Markan version. At Caesarea and Ephesus the local Stories held their ground, though in the end only by consenting to receive Markan supplements.

If we were reconstructing the genesis of the Resurrection tradition entirely from the imagination, we should picture the earliest community anxious to investigate and set out the original facts in detail; but the existing material in the Gospels shows us that this assumption is not warranted. Whether the story of the Visit of the Women to the Tomb was connected with the first Passion Stories, is not easy to decide; what is clear is that the first Christians were satisfied by individual stories of Appearances, told by those who had seen the Risen Lord. Different communities had their own cycles of such stories, Galilean or Judaean in character as the case might be, and when the time came for the task of the chronicler, it was not possible to draw up a continuous historical record. That many saw Jesus, and that the women visited the Tomb were known, but the exact nature of the Resurrection Body of Jesus and the precise succession of events were not known, with the result that our knowledge to-day is limited to what, after all, is the essential thing—traditions of men who affirmed that they saw Jesus after His death. The first Christians cherished such stories, and if some of the narratives bear marks of reflection and defence, the central affirmation is confirmed by the witness of St. Paul and the triumphal march of the Christian Mission.

Besides the Death and Resurrection of Jesus, His

words had an irresistible interest and importance for the
first Christians. Here again the tradition was shaped
by preaching, but also by the manifold experiences of
daily life. Stories which ended in a striking word of
Jesus were often heard in the Christian assemblies, but
they were smoothed and rounded by the action of daily
use and repetition. These stories are especially important because they tell us how the first Christians solved
questions of faith and practice. We see the problems
created by their relations with Judaism, and how they
were met. The first followers of Jesus were Jews, and
they had little desire to make a complete breach with the
faith of their fathers; but obedience to the Message of
Jesus meant a new attitude towards life, and, in consequence, problems arose on every hand. What was to be
their attitude to the Sabbath, to fasting, to food-laws, to
non-Jews, and to notable sinners? How did they stand
in relation to the law of divorce? Were they bound to
pay the Temple-dues? What was to be the future of
Judaism and its Temple? Then there were questions
which arose out of their communal life. What was the
right attitude of a follower of Jesus towards wealth?
Had children a place in Christ's Kingdom? What was
to be done when unauthorized exorcists were undeniably
successful? Questions of faith also confronted them
daily. Unexpected calamities fell upon men, and these
raised the age-long problems of sin and retribution.
Members of the communities died before the Parousia;
what was to be their experience beyond the tomb? The
Kingdom did not come in the way they hoped; when
would Christ return and establish a New Heaven and a

New Earth? Following Jesus entailed sacrifice, the straining of family ties, and sometimes the loss of a settled home; what were His demands in these respects? Finally, they faced, as we face, questions about Jesus Himself. Who were His true kindred? Was He David's Son? Did He work signs and wonders, and what was His attitude thereto? Why were some of His parables hard to understand? Had He authority to forgive sins?

We do not misread the life of the first Christians if we think of them as a reflective people; their situation compelled them to think; but we should certainly be mistaken if we thought of them as a harassed or perplexed people. For if they had problems, they had also a solution; and their solution did not lie in a process of acute reasoning, but in the ready acceptance of the authoritative words of Jesus. It was only when His word seemed ambiguous, or was entirely wanting, that serious difficulties arose, as when questions concerning Gentiles were discussed at the Apostolic Council of Acts xv. For the most part there was little room for uncertainty or friction; their Lord had spoken and His words were spirit and life.

Besides Pronouncement-Stories, the primitive sayings-groups were repeated and taught in the first Christian assemblies, and especially, we may suppose, when young Christians were gathered for purposes of instruction. Free use was also made of isolated sayings, remnants of Pronouncement-Stories in some cases, or words which had lived on apart from discourses which had been forgotten. All these considerations lead us to see

communities supremely interested in the sayings of
Jesus, and to such a degree that the narrative-tradition
suffered. Men were certainly interested in the actions
of Jesus, but they were more interested in His Passion
and in what He had said.

Among the deeds of Jesus first importance was given
to His 'mighty works': Christians loved to dwell on His
compassion and on His victorious conflict with the powers of darkness, and for this reason healing-stories and
accounts of exorcisms were told and retold. Christians
believed that nothing, not even death, could withstand
the might of Jesus; but the rarity of stories of raising
from the dead and of nature-miracles shows how little
they were inclined to invest Him with powers of magic.
Apart from Miracle-Stories, they were interested in
narratives which told of decisive moments in the life of
Jesus and in incidents which pictured His habitual in-
tercourse with men and reflected ideas precious to the
communities. The stories cherished were those which
told how He was anointed for His Mission, how He was
tempted, how He called and chose His disciples, how He
was rejected by His fellow-countrymen, how His Messiahship was recognized but only partially understood,
how He was authenticated by God on the Mount of
Transfiguration, and how He came to His Passion and
Death. For the rest, the stories loved were those which
revealed His attitude to sinners, the nature of His Message, and His dealings with individual men and women.

Throughout the whole of this first period no sign of a
demand meets us for a connected record, apart from the
Passion Story, and no interest is visible in the life of

Jesus earlier than His Ministry.   The time is one in which precious fragments are treasured for their immediate interest and value; Christian hands are full of jewels, but there is no desire to weave a crown.   This does not mean that a knowledge of the course of events was wholly lost; the Gospel of Mark shows that this was not the case; but it does mean that, as a chain of connected events, the primitive reminiscences were not valued in the way we should have supposed.   To the modern man this is surprising, for it is so easy for us to think that what is of the greatest interest to us must have been highly esteemed in those first days.   We need not doubt that the first Christians listened with deep interest to Peter and others as they told how one thing followed another; but if the succession of events had been for them a matter of great importance it would be far better represented in the Gospels than it is.   The first period is one in which the self-contained story, the sayings-group, and the single saying represent the normal types of tradition and the prevailing range of interest.

II

The second period extends approximately from about 50 to 65 A.D., though some of the processes now to be described may have begun in the earlier period.   The characteristic mark of this second stage is the attempt to gather the scattered elements of the tradition into groups.   This development does not seem to have included the Narrative-tradition, except that the enlargement of the Passion Stories may still have been in progress.   The new departure concerned rather the sayings of Jesus. The material was arranged in topical rather than chronological succession for purposes of Christian instruction and defence.

In this endeavour attention was naturally directed to the Pronouncement-Stories. Could not these stories be arranged in such a way as to promote instruction, and to serve the ends of attack and defence in the face of hostile Jewish criticisms? In isolation the stories had proved to be valuable; might they not be still more effective in combination?

These are not idle suppositions; the existing material in the Gospels suggests that the first Christians adopted this plan. It is tempting to find an illustration in Mk. vii. 1-23, where a Pronouncement-Story and a group of sayings form a complex dealing with questions of ritual uncleanness and obedience to the traditions of the Elders; but this arrangement may well be the work of Mark when he composed his Gospel for the Roman Christians who had an interest in these questions (cf. Rom. xiv.). Mark may also have associated the story of the Kindred of Jesus with that of the Beelzebub Controversy; for in the one story the words 'He is beside himself' are paralleled by the cry 'He hath Beelzebub' in the other (iii. 21f.). What, however, we are looking for is not the Evangelist's literary methods, but signs of a like purpose in the pre-Gospel period, the results of which Mark took over and embodied in his work. As I have indicated in an earlier lecture (cf. p. 16), it is the merit of Albertz' investigation that it gives us good reason to think that such primitive collections actually existed.

The cohesion of Mk. ii. 1-iii. 6 has long been noted, but Albertz (*S.S.* 5-16) has carried his observations further.   As we have seen, this section consists of five Pronouncement-Stories, loosely joined together.   Albertz has pointed out that in these five stories there is a gradual mounting of the opposition between Jesus and the Pharisees which reaches its climax in iii. 6.   In the first story, that of the Paralytic, the opposition is latent; the scribes reason within themselves: 'Why doth this man thus speak? he blasphemeth: who can forgive sins but one, even God?' (ii. 7).   In the second story an objection against Jesus is voiced, but in the hearing of the disciples: 'He eateth with publicans and sinners' (ii. 16). In the third Jesus is questioned, but about an omission on the part of His disciples who do not fast like the disciples of John and of the Pharisees (ii. 18), while in the fourth story, in a way that suggests His responsibility, He is challenged with their breach of the Law: 'Behold, why do they on the sabbath day that which is not lawful?' (ii. 24).   In the last story Jesus Himself is watched with hostile intent (iii. 2), and the series closes with the words: 'And the Pharisees went out, and straightway with the Herodians took counsel against him, how they might destroy him' (iii. 6).

Obviously, the section has been carefully and deliberately compiled.   But this is not all.   Albertz reminds us, and indeed this has often been noticed, that the words just quoted come much too early in Mark's plan. No immediate attempt is made to carry out the plot, and later in the same chapter scribes are among His hearers.   Would Mark have introduced the statement

M

in iii. 6 at this point, if he had been writing freely? A
further point of great importance is that the section
contains two references to the 'Son of man' (ii. 10, 28).
Every student of the Gospels knows the difficulties
which these two passages raise, for there is no other reference to the Son of man until after the great day at
Caesarea Philippi, when Peter confesses: 'Thou art the
Christ' (viii. 29). Thenceforward, and with evident intention, Mark introduces the term no less than twelve
times, and generally in the closest association with
Jesus's Mission. It was, of course, on this account
that Wellhausen suggested that the phrase 'Son of man'
in ii. 10 and 28 is the mistranslation of the Aramaic
original which simply read 'man'. Wellhausen's suggestion is very attractive, but the position is entirely
altered if Albertz' new hypothesis is right, for on this
view all the difficulties fall into place.

Albertz suggests that Mark himself did not compile
the section; it was the work of an earlier compiler who
wanted to illustrate the way in which the breach between
Jesus and the religious and political leaders of His day
was effected. Hence the gradual mounting of the opposition, hence the final reference to the plot, and hence
the use of the term 'Son of man' which the compiler was
entirely free to employ! What Mark does is to take
over this complex, either from a document or from oral
tradition; in a conservative spirit he weaves it into his
Gospel (cf. ii. 1 and 13), even though it does not entirely suit his plan. It is significant that this collection
reveals the same interest in the Death of Jesus which
marks the Passion Story; the first Christians wanted to

know, and to show, how it was that Jesus came to His Cross.

Albertz (*S.S.* 16-36) points to a second example, similar in kind, in Mk. xi. 15-7, 27-33, xii. 13-40. Here again are five Pronouncement-Stories: Authority (xi. 27-33), Tribute-Money (xii. 13-7), the Question about the Resurrection (xii. 18-27), the Great Commandment (xii. 28-34), and the Question about David's Son (xii. 35-7). The five are introduced by the story of the Cleansing (xi. 15-7) and are followed by the warning against the Pharisees (xii. 38-40) which may, Albertz suggests, have been added by Mark himself. When we think of it, there is a certain artificiality of form in the succession of the various deputations; while the picture of Jesus as a Teacher, unequalled in His success, popular with the crowd, and victorious over all His adversaries is not quite that of Mk. x. 32ff., according to which Jesus goes to Jerusalem to suffer and to die. All the stories are historical, and probably belong to an advanced stage in the Ministry; they are also rightly associated with Jerusalem and the Temple; but one wonders if they do not belong to an earlier visit which Mark does not record, and if the arrangement itself is not that of an earlier compiler.[1] Albertz suggests that Mark has provided the group with 'lights which illuminate the way to the Passion' in the reference to the Priests' Plot in xi. 18 (cf. xii. 12) and the parable of the Vineyard (xii. 1-11)

[1] Having always preferred the Johannine date of the Cleansing (Jn. ii. 13-22), I am naturally interested in the possibility that here we may have a suggestion of the way in which Mark comes to associate this event with the Last Week.

which certainly seems to be inserted in its present context. He points out that the issue raised in the collection is that of 'Jesus or the Rabbis?' and ingeniously suggests that it may be the work of some one belonging to the circle of Stephen.

Like the early Passion Stories, these groups illustrate the first stages in the process of Gospel compilation; we see that, for all its originality, Mark was not a work begun *de novo*, but a composition which gathered into itself earlier attempts to serve religious and apologetic needs. It is eloquent both of the primitive nature of Mark, and of the conservatism of its author, that we can still trace in it indications of an earlier period. When we compare the form given to the two pre-Markan groups in Matthew and Luke, we see that a more literary spirit is at work which reshapes the material and supplies temporal and local connecting-links, so that the record becomes a literary whole. Grateful as we are for this, the literary gain would be historical loss if we did not possess Mark. It is of still greater importance that the primitive groups give us glimpses of the life and thoughts of the first Christians. In both collections Jesus stands in the centre, victorious over his enemies who nevertheless are unrelenting in their endeavours to bear Him down. The means adopted to supply this representation are of the simplest; they consist of nothing more than the stringing together of stories which had circulated singly in the primitive community. Pronouncement-Stories are arranged topically for purposes of teaching and defence.

More important than the combining of Pronouncement-Stories was the formation of sayings-collections during the period under review. I am afraid we cannot say much about the Markan collection, except that it consisted of isolated sayings strung together for catechetical purposes. More can be inferred regarding the origin of Q, for this source is used in two of our Gospels and has long been the object of study and investigation. The primary data for the student are the linguistic agreements in Matthew and Luke; but something can also be contributed by viewing the problems from the standpoint of form and especially in connexion with conclusions which we have already reached.

Divergence of opinion regarding Q is sometimes referred to as if it were a matter for reproach. There is, of course, no doubt about the divergence of view. B. W. Bacon, for example, is sure that Q contained a Passion-narrative and was in fact a Gospel (*Studies in Matthew*, 1930, p. 214f.), and similar opinions have been put forward by F. C. Burkitt, J. V. Bartlet, and others. On the other hand, P. Wernle (*Die synoptische Frage*, 1899, p. 225) holds that the source contained brief sayings alone, while very many critics, including J. C. Hawkins, W. Sanday, and B. H. Streeter, maintain that, in addition to sayings, Q included only a few stories like the Temptation and the Centurion's Servant and short introductory passages. At the moment we are faced with a theory of W. Bussmann (*S.Sn.* ii. 110-56) which suggests that Q is a fusion of two documents, one written in Greek (T) which contained narratives and sayings, and the other written in Aramaic (R) containing sayings exclusively. The object of this theory is to account for

passages where the agreement between Matthew and
Luke is high, and also for other parallel passages where
the agreement is low. The solution is attractive because
it covers many facts, and because Bussmann can point to
many examples of what appear to be translation-variants;
but the hypothesis has yet to pass through the fires of
debate. In particular, it will be necessary to compare it
with Streeter's alternative theory, that Luke restricts himself to Q in cases where Matthew conflates Q and M.

There is point in mentioning these differences of
opinion because their number and variety suggests a
door of hope. May it not be that many of the investigators are right, at least in their affirmations? I suggest
that something like this is indicated by our present study
of the formative process.

The delusion that prevents all progress is the assumption that Q remained one and the same entity over a
number of years. It is because this is so often assumed
that critical views are so various: the investigators describe the source at different points in its complex history. Although Q was the work of an individual, it
was rooted in the life of primitive Christianity, and its
fortunes must have reflected the circumstances of its
origins: it changed, as it was bound to change, because
it was responsive to the life it fed.

The simplest and most natural view is that Q began
as a sayings-source pure and simple. The fragmentary
narrative element in most reconstructions of its contents
suggests this, and the inference is supported by the
broad probabilities of the case. Q was an innovation
prompted by the needs of catechetical instruction. The

times demanded a compend of the Lord's oracles, similar in form to the wise sayings of the Book of Proverbs. Such a collection could take its rise only out of that which already existed, and it was compiled from Pronouncement-Stories, sayings-groups, and words of Jesus in free circulation. The sayings in the Pronouncement-Stories may be compared with plants to which some of the soil still clings: Q was a chaplet of gathered flowers, found singly or in clusters. As such, it was treasured for its fragrance and its value. But Q could not escape the circumstances of its origins. Wherever it was carried, it existed in communities which still possessed Pronouncement-Stories, sayings, parables, and narratives about Jesus; and, in consequence, supplementation of the primitive document must have begun at a very early time. To some extent we may compare the textual fortunes of the Latin Vulgate which pursued its victorious way, but only by consenting to change; ancient readings found their way back until a mixed text came into general use. The same process can be observed in hymn-books which replace earlier collections. The simplest explanation of Q, as we see it in the Gospels, is that already it had admitted Pronouncement-Stories like the Baptist's Question, Stories about Jesus like the Temptation and the Centurion's Servant, and parables like the Great Supper and the Pounds; and some of these in variant forms in the different communities which used the source.

Traces of the expansion of Q are more easily found in Luke than in Matthew, for the First Evangelist carried forward the catechetical purpose which gave it birth; he agglutinated sayings, combining them with those of other collections (Mark and M), and arranged the whole in five sections comparable to the five Books of the Law. Q, however, as used by Matthew, presupposes expansions, as, for example, in the parables of the Marriage Feast (xxii. 1ff.). Caesarea followed a different course, preserving for the most part the original order of Q, and respecting its linguistic forms, but none the less making additions which transformed the document until it cried out to be made into a type of primitive Gospel. Proto-Luke itself was only the more ambitious extension of a process which had already begun. Is not this process illustrated in the Lukan expansions of the story of the Centurion's Servant? Here the elders commend the officer to Jesus as one that 'loveth our nation, and himself built us our synagogue', and when Jesus approaches he sends his friends to meet Him out of a sense of personal unworthiness (vii. 6f.). In like manner the story of the Despatch and Return of the Seventy (x. 1, 17-20) appears to be an expansion of the Mission Charge as it stood in the first draft of Q. The full tale of facts which would permit this hypothesis to be demonstrated is hidden from us, yet enough evidence exists to make it probable that, just as single stories and small groups came into existence by stages, so Q is a source which grew and in its growth foreshadowed a development ultimately completed in the Gospels.

The time has not yet come when we can tell the story that lies behind the M Source. Both Streeter and Bussmann have given us reason to think that it was a late source, and, if it is a unity, the character of its parables and of some of its sayings supports this view; but our investigation has suggested that it also contained sayings-groups in which both the arrangement and the sayings are primitive. The L source was first committed to writing by Luke; it contained material of every kind—a Passion Story, Pronouncement-Stories, sayings, Miracle-Stories, and Stories about Jesus. In both M and L the special interests of very different communities are clearly manifest, and each in different ways contributes to our understanding of the teaching of Jesus and the history of the primitive tradition.[1]

III

The third period, that of Gospel compilation, covers the rest of the century from about 65 A.D. There is no breach between this period and the preceding one; for, on a much larger scale, the Evangelists carried forward the work of those who first grouped Pronouncement-Stories and expanded Q. In this development they were not alone, as Luke indicates when he speaks of 'many' who had 'taken in hand to draw up a narrative' (i. 1). A special impulse to the task of Gospel compilation was given by the rapid expansion of the Gentile Mission, the lapse of time, and the increased need for Christian instruction and defence.

The story of the writing of the Gospels has often been told and need not be repeated here except in so far as it concerns our present investigation.

Luke, I believe, was the first of our four Evangelists to begin the larger undertaking. The expansion which

[1]This is well illustrated by T. W. Manson in *The Teaching of Jesus*.

Q had already undergone suggested to him the idea of a still further enlargement which consisted of the addition to Q of the Passion Story and the local narrative- and discourse-tradition of Caesarea. The first-fruits of this plan was a sketch of the Ministry of Jesus which we can still trace behind the Third Gospel; but the undertaking was premature, and there is no reason to think that Proto-Luke was ever published. Luke had the greatness which can withhold a historical work from publicity until it is complete. Only when he was able to supplement the first draft by copious extracts from Mark and by his own superb idyll of the Nativity, was he ready to despatch it to Theophilus in order that he, and doubtless others too, might know the certainty concerning the things in which they had been instructed (i. 4). This larger purpose was effected probably in the early eighties. I will only add that such a picture of literary activity, which carries forward earlier attempts at Gospel compilation and is at first quite tentative, seems to me to be entirely in keeping with the practice of a writer who, during the Pauline Mission, had begun to keep the diary which forms the basis of the second part of the Acts, and it is also in line with the earlier stages we have observed in the formation of the Gospel tradition.

Mark's task is also illuminated by our earlier studies. Writing at Rome between 65 and 70 A.D., Mark had unique advantages. A native of Jerusalem, he knew the popular tradition of Palestine; a resident at Rome, he had access to the local discourse-tradition of the Roman Church; a former 'attendant' of Peter, he had at his disposal memories of Peter's preaching. The Petrine stories and a knowledge of the progress of events derived from Peter, supplied him with an outline into which he inserted single stories and small collections of primitive material in such a way as to show how Jesus, the Messiah, came to His Passion and His Cross.   The links with earlier stages are unmistakable.   Mark is not a skilled writer; and the development of his Story is due, not so much to his editorial powers and doctrinal ideas, as to the tradition he knew and the special advantages he enjoyed.

The work of the First Evangelist gave fuller expression to the catechetical purpose which guided the formation of the earlier sayings-collections.   But Matthew was also responsive to the historical interests which animated Luke; he wanted to relate the teaching of Jesus to the story of His Life, and it was on this account that he re-edited and expanded Mark.   So successfully did he achieve this purpose, that it is no matter for wonder that from the second century onwards his writing was the favourite Gospel in the early Church and is quoted more freely than any other.   The paucity and the inferior character of its special narrative-tradition support the views of those who find the place of composition outside Palestine, in Antioch or North Syria, and date the Gospel about 90 A.D.   Unlike Luke, Matthew does not attempt to give a full account of the Nativity, but contents himself with recording a few late apologetic stories and a Genealogy designed to show that Jesus was the adopted Son of Joseph.   From the standpoint of the modern critic, the First Gospel is the least valuable of the Synoptics, but none the less its importance is very great because it includes within itself several streams of testimony, and because it has much to tell us about the period in which it was compiled. Its author was a Churchman who wrote in the belief that Jesus came in the order of God's providential purpose to establish a New Law and a Kingdom of Righteousness.

The Fourth Gospel presents the Gospel tradition at the peak of its development. Written at the end of the first century, it embodies a tradition which, I believe, is in some way connected with the Apostle John, but the actual author is not known. To-day, the Gospel is often attributed to the Elder John named by Papias, but all that we know of this enigmatic figure warns us that he is not likely to have been the author. Whoever the Evangelist was, he gives us the tradition in the form it came to assume in his mind after many years of thought and experience. But while this is so, our study as a whole suggests that we ought not to distinguish too sharply between the Evangelist and the community for which he wrote. If the form of the narratives and sayings owes much to his hand, it is also probable that the shaping process had long been in progress, and that his readers had become accustomed to, and appreciated, its peculiar stamp. It is the work of the Evangelist, but it is also the tradition of Ephesus, the form of the Gospel Story which met its needs, answered its questions, and informed its Christianity.

Such, then, is the reconstruction suggested by our study of the formation of the Gospel tradition. If, in many ways, it confirms conclusions already widely held, this is all to the good, because they are seen to be more firmly grounded; but I hope it has also opened out possibilities which enrich our knowledge of the tradition and of its history.   Far more than Form Criticism is needed to enable us to trace out this history, but real help is afforded by this method and useful contributions are made.   If there are points where our perplexity is deepened rather than removed, we have no right to complain, for that is inevitable in any inquiry.   But the main result, I believe, is not deeper mystery, but fuller understanding.   We see Jesus better, for we behold Him, not only in the final form which the tradition assumes in the Gospels, but also in the lives, thoughts, and desires of men throughout the formative period.   We are also enabled to appreciate the Gospels better, for we see earlier forms and stages out of which they emerged, and are enabled to mark the influences which shaped their growth.   How great are these works with such a history behind them!   Far from losing the idea of Inspiration, we are led to see that the Spirit of God must have been at work upon a grander scale, not coercing men or using them as blind instruments, but elevating their minds to perceive, to transmit, and to interpret the best elements in the tradition.   Literature has no books which can justly be compared with the Gospels, which indeed come to us from men, but in the last analysis are the gifts of God, seals of His grace and sacraments of His love.

APPENDIX A

THE PROTO-LUKE HYPOTHESIS AND SOME RECENT CRITICISM

IN view of my references to the Proto-Luke Hypothesis on pp. 6f, 51f, it is necessary to consider the criticisms of Canon Creed in his stimulating commentary, *The Gospel according to St. Luke* (1930), especially as it is claimed in the present lectures that Proto-Luke finds its natural place in the story of the formation of the Gospel tradition.

Canon Creed's main criticisms are set forth in an important footnote on p. lviii of his commentary (cf. also pp. lxiv, 86, 140, 253, 262, 274). His primary objection to the Proto-Luke Hypothesis is that 'whereas Mark appears to give a clue to the disposition of "Proto-Luke" in the existing Gospel, the subtraction of Markan material leaves an amorphous collection of narrative and discourse the greater part of which is thrown without intelligible reason into the unsuitable form of a "travel document" (ix. 52–xviii.)'.

If in this extract the word "Proto-Luke" were printed without inverted commas, the first positive objection would not be of serious importance. For to admit that Mk. iii. 13-9 (The Choice of the Twelve) and Mk. x. 1 (The Departure from Galilee) give a clue to the disposition of Proto-Luke in the Third Gospel, would not

necessarily mean that Mark was Luke's fundamental
source; and, in any case, the existence of Proto-Luke
would be admitted. But I take it that by "Proto-Luke"
Canon Creed means the contents of this 'source', and
that by the word 'clue' he means that, with Mark before
us, we can account for the disposal of Q and L material
in the Third Gospel. This does not seem to me to be
true. It is always Q, in combination with L material,
which stands in Markan contexts, and the parallel to any
omitted Markan section is very often found in a completely different context from the one suggested by the
Markan outline. These facts lead us to think that Q + L,
or Proto-Luke, was an entity, in the form of a document,
at the time when the Third Gospel was composed.

The negative objection contained in the passage
quoted above, does not appear to be any more formid-
able. If the account of the formation of the Gospel
tradition which I have given is sound, an 'amorphous
collection' of narrative and discourse, compiled in the
period 60-5 A.D., is not an anomaly; such a collection
could not well be anything else than 'amorphous', unless
the compiler had enjoyed advantages like those of
Mark through his association with Peter. To say that
the collection 'is thrown without intelligible reason into
the unsuitable form of a "travel document" ', is to mis-
conceive the conditions of the primitive period, when
a knowledge of the succession of events was hard to
gain, because for a generation it had not been an object
of interest.[1] In such circumstances an Evangelist had

[1]'What the historian has to explain, in a community of Jewish origin,
is not the existence of amorphous collections—which was the normal

to do the best he could.   Luke's procedure is not unintelligible; it was suggested to him partly by the nature of his material (cf. the Samaritan Village, ix. 52*b*-6; and the Mission Charge, x. 2-12), and partly by his conviction that the journey to Jerusalem which preceded the Passion was a period of outstanding importance in the Story of Jesus.

Canon Creed naturally devotes attention to the signs of the use of Mark in the Third Gospel, and refers, in particular, to Lk. iii. 3, iii. 16 (cited as probable), and to a number of passages in the Passion-narrative.

The first two passages appear in Lk. iii. 1–iv. 30, which is claimed by supporters of the Proto-Luke Hypothesis as a non-Markan section.   I have already replied to Archdeacon J. W. Hunkin's objections to this view in the *Journal of Theological Studies* (Apr. 1927, Jan. 1928), and will content myself here with a brief reference to the main points.   The words, 'preaching the baptism of repentance unto remission of sins' in Lk. iii. 3, together with the phrases, 'the latchet of whose shoes', and 'to unloose', in Lk. iii. 16, represent practically the sole linguistic foundation on which to base the view that Luke wrote iii. 1–iv. 30 with Mk. i. 1-15 before him.   This basis is meagre enough; but it is still more doubtful when it is remembered that the agreements might be accidental, or might be traced to Q, or might be details added from Mark at the time when Proto-Luke was expanded to form the Third Gospel.   It seems to me to be precarious to found an

thing—but the emergence of a non-amorphous biography like Mark'
(B. H. Streeter, *F.G.*, 4th impression, 1930, p. xiiif.).

N

objection to the Proto-Luke Hypothesis on such points, which need rather to be decided in the light of the problem as a whole.

But it is to the Lukan Passion-narrative that Canon Creed gives fuller consideration. Here, he reminds us, 'not only are there complete sections which are unmistakably taken from Mark (*e.g.* xxii. 7-13, 54-61), but Markan phrases appear in the middle of sections which in other respects differ considerably from Mark (see *e.g.* xxii. 19*a*, 22, 47, 52, 71; xxiii. 3)'. The point at issue, of course, is the significance of this use of Mark, and Canon Creed expounds this by saying: 'These signs of Mark are intelligible if the Lukan narrative is a recasting and expansion of the Markan text'. I feel very doubtful about this explanation, because most of the passages which betray their Markan origin, at all events in Lk. xxii. 14–xxiv. 11, are details or matters of secondary importance.[1] But even if Canon Creed's claim were just, the question would still remain: Are not the signs of Mark still more intelligible if the Lukan narrative has been expanded by extracts from Mark? This vital question he answers as follows: 'If, however, Luke had already written or found a full and independent non-Markan narrative, it seems unlikely that afterwards he would have interpolated occasional sentences and verses from Mark'. This is indeed a strange way of settling a complicated critical problem! Why should the procedure described be thought unlikely? Surely, if Luke had written an independent

---

[1]See the list of 'Markan insertions' printed on p. 51. The story of the Denial would be the exception.

narrative of the Passion, and then later found new and
interesting information in Mark's Gospel, it would be
the most natural thing in the world to insert extracts from
such an authority into his own story. Not to do so would
be inconsistent with the claims of his Preface (Lk. i.
1-4). For this reason it does not seem open to Canon
Creed forthwith to say: 'It appears to me, therefore, that
Mark must be regarded as a determining factor in the
construction of the existing book from the outset'. His
concluding observation might even be conceived as
tantamount to an acceptance of the hypothesis against
which he contends: 'This, however, is not necessarily inconsistent with the hypothesis that Q and some of Luke's
peculiar material may have been already combined, and
may have lain before Luke as a single document'.

On p. lxiv Canon Creed refers to the twelve transpositions in the order of incidents and paragraphs
which raise such difficulties, if Mark is the primary
source.[1] He attributes the chief of them to 'Luke's
own historical criticism', but on the same page he
quotes with approval and in italics, the well-known
opinion of Sir John C. Hawkins that the transpositions
'suggest a long and gradual conflation in the mind
rather than a simple conflation by the pen' (*O.S.* 90).
If these two views are to be taken together, the 'historical criticism' must have been of long standing at the
time when the Third Gospel was compiled. But, as I
have pointed out on p. 51, of the twelve transpositions
seven involve passages which have been taken from
Mark (Lk. xxii. 19*a*, 22, 34, 54*b*-61; xxiii. 38, 45, 54),

[1]See earlier, p. 52.

and the curious thing is that these passages stand in Luke and in Mark in the same order, with the exception of the first (cf. Mk. xiv. 22, 21, 30, 66-72; xv. 26, 38, 42). This fact is hardly consistent with the idea of 'a long and gradual conflation in the mind'; Luke must have consulted his Markan source at the time when he introduced these passages into his Gospel. This inference is confirmed when it is seen that other Markan passages (Lk. xxii. 46*b* (?), 50*b*, 52-3*a*; xxiii. 3, 26, 34*b* (?), 44, 50-3; xxiv. 10 (?)) are also in the Markan succession (Mk. xiv. 38, 47, 48f.; xv. 2, 21, 24*b*, 33, 43-7; xvi. 1). Is not the simplest explanation found in the view that, when Luke wrote his Gospel, Mark was consulted in the actual process of writing, and that one by one all the above passages were added to Proto-Luke, with the not unnatural result that in seven cases the insertions had to be made in contexts which did not agree with those of Mark? If this is so, preference ought to be given to the earlier opinion of Sir John Hawkins, that the Passion-narrative contains the strongest argument in favour of Feine's theory, that 'Luke had before him some kind of record, or early Gospel', other than Mark and Q. It also follows that if the term 'historical criticism' can be used of his task, Luke's criticism is to be seen in his preference for Proto-Luke, as supplemented by Mark, and not in the theory that what he did was to rewrite, re-arrange, and enlarge Mark's account (cf. Creed, *St. Luke*, 262).

Another point of considerable importance is that the Markan passages, in relation to their Lukan context, have the appearance of being secondary strata. I have instanced many cases of this (*B.T.G.* 34-67), but the only one which Canon Creed examines is perhaps the weakest example.   With reference to Lk. xxii. 52-3, I have argued that the greater part of 52-3*a* ('Are ye come out as against a robber? . . .') is a Markan addition, and that in Proto-Luke Jesus said to 'the captains of the temple', 'This is your hour, and the power of darkness'.   Canon Creed observes: 'But the words could not stand alone: they demand the contrast of the Markan sentence which precedes' (*op. cit.*, 274).   'Demand' seems to me much too strong a word, for the reply could be provoked by the arrest itself.   But this is one of the cases where one cannot pretend to be able to recover the original text of Proto-Luke exactly.   As examples where the issue is unambiguous, xxii. 19*a*, 22, 54*b*-61; xxiii. 3, 26, 38, 44f., 50-4 should be examined; and here, I think, it will be found that the Lukan narrative loses little in coherence, and in some cases actually gains, if the Markan passages are omitted.   This is strange indeed, if 'Mark must be regarded as a determining factor in the construction of the existing book from the outset'.[1]

---

[1] I feel sure that Canon Creed unintentionally misrepresents my linguistic argument when he says: 'Dr. Taylor's numerical method of dealing with the words peculiar to each evangelist is not satisfactory without reference to the actual similarities and dissimilarities in each case' (*op. cit.* 86*n*).   In *Behind the Third Gospel* I have discussed this very peril (cf. pp. 29-32), and, so far as I know, have never made use of computations and percentages without reference to 'the actual similarities and dissimilarities in each case'.   In discussing the passage to which the footnote is attached (Lk. vi. 12-9), I devote three pages to such discussions (*B.T.G.* 81-3).   Canon Creed does not use the numerical method at all, and the result is that from his commentary it is very difficult to estimate Luke's debt to Mark.

I cannot think that Canon Creed has succeeded in shaking those arguments in favour of the Proto-Luke Hypothesis to which he devotes attention; but there are also others to which he does not give sufficient consideration. Luke's omission of about half of Mark's Gospel is an example. Many explanations have been advanced for what is a peculiar circumstance, if Mark is the foundation source. Canon Creed repeats many of these, but places his main reliance on the theory that 'Luke clearly avoids doublets'. I have no doubt that this explanation goes a long way towards a solution of the problem, but, in view of W. Bussmann's recent demonstration that Luke uses more doublets than any other Evangelist (*Synoptische Studien*, i. 56-63), it does not adequately account for the facts. On the Proto-Luke Hypothesis, the difficulties disappear, since, on this theory, Luke takes from Mark only what he needs to supplement Proto-Luke.

Among the points which Canon Creed has not discussed are: (1) the significance of the alternation of blocks of non-Markan and Markan matter; (2) the fact that the non-Markan sections are relatively continuous, while the Markan sections are self-contained, and supply the deficiencies of Proto-Luke; (3) Luke's use of Q, which stands apart from Markan matter, but is combined with L; (4) the fact that the hypothesis easily finds room for peculiar features in the Gospel, such as the date in iii. 1f., the position of the Genealogy (iii. 23-38), and the prominence given to the Visit to Nazareth (iv. 16-30); and (5) the harmony of the hypothesis both with the implications of the Preface (i. 1-4), and with Luke's literary methods in the Acts (cf. *B.T.G.* 182-202; *G.* 40-5).

It is important to discuss all these issues, because the hypothesis is one of those theories which are accepted, if at all, because they account for a considerable number of facts taken as a whole. The problem is certainly affected if one or a few of these facts can be otherwise explained; but only if many of them demand other explanations, and if evidence of an unfavourable character can be found, must the hypothesis be abandoned and replaced. It is hardly too much to say that so far the opposition has not proved to be more than a matter of isolated raids and attacks on outposts.

Much the same is true of continental discussions. Klostermann's attitude of reserve is not supported by any arguments, and relates to the L source rather than to the Proto-Luke Hypothesis (cf. *Das Lukasevangelium*, 2nd ed. 1929, p. 49). Bussmann treats a few points only. In discussing Parts I and II of his *Synoptische Studien* in an extended review (*H.J.*, July 1931, pp. 757-60), I expressed the opinion that his theory of Luke's use of Mark is really an alternative to the Proto-Luke Hypothesis. Part III fully justified this opinion (cf. *H.J.*, Jan. 1932, pp. 378-80). Bussmann has argued that three stages can be traced in the composition of Mark: a short form (G) known to Luke, a longer form (B) used by Matthew, and the Canonical Gospel (E). It is obvious that a critic who holds this view will not be likely to welcome the Proto-Luke Hypothesis, because he has otherwise explained Luke's use of Mark. This, I think, goes far to explain his rejection of Proto-Luke, and the piecemeal character of his objections. He claims that the hypothesis is not supported by Lk. i. 1-4, that Luke's Markan omissions are best explained by his own theory of the origin of Mark, that the use of ὁ κύριος and κύριε (in Proto-Luke) may be Luke's stylistic alterations, and that Canon Streeter's claim that two periods of Luke's literary activity are discernible in the Gospel, as in the Acts, fails because we need to distinguish between Luke and the *auctor ad Theophilum* (cf. *S.Sn.*, iii. 136-41). Of these arguments only the first two seriously affect the issue, and the first hardly survives a perusal of the Lukan Preface:

> 'Forasmuch as many have taken in hand to draw up a narrative . . ., it seemed good to me also, having traced the course of all things accurately from the first, to write unto thee in order, most excellent Theophilus . . .'.

If Proto-Luke was never published, Luke was under no obligation to mention it; and if, on the other hand, it was a first draft of the Gospel, he could, with added justice, claim to have 'traced the course of all things accurately from the first'.

Bussmann's theory of Luke's use of Mark is an extension of the *Ur-Markus* hypothesis. It is impossible to discuss this completely now, and it is perhaps unnecessary, inasmuch as the *Ur-Markus* theory has fallen into general discredit (cf. *F.G.* 331). But Bussmann's onslaught on the view that 'Luke clearly avoids doublets' is so thorough and convincing that, in rejecting his theory of three stages in the composition of Mark, critics will probably find themselves well on the way to the acceptance of the Proto-Luke Hypothesis.

I conclude with a reference to a criticism which was made by Dr. W. K. Lowther Clarke in *Theology* (July 1926, pp. 46-9). Dr. Clarke wrote: 'The advocates of the new theory have not, so it seems, studied the bearing of recent German Synoptic criticism upon their conclusions'.[1] This omission has now been made good in the preceding Lectures. I think it will be seen that Proto-Luke readily falls into place in the story of the formation of the Gospel tradition which Form-Criticism enables us to trace. It is perhaps an advantage that the Proto-Luke Hypothesis was first stated apart from such studies; for we now see that if this hypothesis had not been formulated, we should need to suggest something like it, as a kind of intermediate stage between the Canonical Gospels, on the one hand, and the conditions of the primitive period, on the other hand, when the tradition consisted of isolated narratives and small groups of sayings, followed in course of time by short collections framed to meet the growing needs of early Christianity.

[1] Recently in principle and in substance the Proto-Luke Hypothesis has been advocated by J. Jeremias, *The Eucharistic Words of Jesus* (1955), pp. 69f, *New Testament Studies*, ' Perikopen- Umstellungen bei Lukas?' vol. 4, 115-19, H. Schürmann, *Der Paschamahlbericht* also *Jesu Abschiedsrede* (1957), p. 140f, F. Rehkopf, *Die lukanische Sonderquelle* (1959). See also my article ' Methods of Gospel Criticism', *The Expository Times*, vol. lxxi (Dec. 1959), and *The Gospels: A Short Introduction* (1960), p. 43.

APPENDIX B

THE TENDENCIES OF ORAL TRANSMISSION

CONSIDERATIONS of space make it impossible to give a full account of the experiments referred to on p. 124, but a brief selection from the evidence is desirable, in order to indicate its character and the reasonableness of the conclusions. While no experiments can reproduce the conditions of the Gospel period, it should be possible to discover what are the tendencies of oral transmission; and this knowledge, if it can be gained, is useful in evaluating the Gospel narratives.

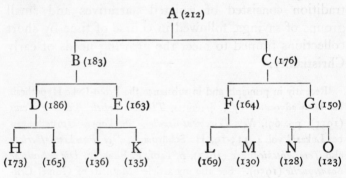

In the experiments, an original story (A) was traced through three stages of transmission. The results at the first remove are represented by B and C. At the second remove, they are shown by D and E, which depend on B; and by F and G, which depend on C. At the third remove from A, there are eight versions: H and I (from D), J and K (from E), L and M (from F), and N and O (from G). In the above table, the relationship of the different versions is set out, the number of words in each case being indicated.

The original story (A) was chosen for its detail and the presence of direct speech, and is as follows:

'One night, towards sunset, Rabbi ben Simon was meditating on the roof of his house, which was situated in the outskirts of Joppa. Enwrapped in his thoughts, he did not notice the lapse of time, until at length he fell asleep. About the end of the first watch, he was awakened by a voice. "Come, Rabbi ben Simon", cried the voice, "to the house of thy friend, Rabbi Eleazer, for great grief has fallen upon it". Walking to the edge of the roof, ben Simon peered down into the faint light, and saw a form huddled at the foot of the stairs. "Who art thou?", he cried, "speak, for I am here". The messenger was astonished to find ben Simon awake and fully clothed, but hastened to tell of the sudden sickness and swift death which had come upon his friend. "Alas!", cried ben Simon, "What shall I do? The hour is late, and the journey far!". But his hesitation was short, for he saw that it was not well for one who walked by the Torah to delay good deeds. "Wait", he said, "I will come with thee". Taking then a staff only, he descended from his house, and hasted by the sea-shore to the stricken house of his friend.'

Instead of reproducing all the versions of this story, I will give, as typical of the whole, the two series: B, E, J, and C, G, N. The more important additions are shown by italics.

B (from A):

I

'One evening near the time of sunset Rabbi ben Simon was seated meditating on the roof of his house, which was on the outskirts of Joppa. He was so wrapped up in his thoughts that he did not notice the lapse of time. Suddenly he heard a voice: "Come, Rabbi ben Simon, and *behold* the grief that has fallen upon the house of thy friend, Rabbi Eleazer". Surprised, he walked to the edge of the roof, and peered into the half light, and beheld a figure huddled at the foot of the stairs. "Who art thou?", he said. The messenger, surprised to find Rabbi ben Simon already there, could only say: "Come, and behold the great grief and sudden death that has fallen upon the house of thy friend". "Alas! What shall I do?", cried Rabbi ben Simon, "for the hour is late". But his hesitation was only for a moment, for he knew well that he who walks by the Torah should not delay in good works. Taking down a staff, he walked by the sea to the house of Rabbi Eleazer.'

E (from B):

'One evening about the time of sunset, Rabbi ben Simon sat meditating on the roof of his house, which was *beside the sea* on the outskirts of Joppa. He was so absorbed in his thoughts that he did not notice the lapse of time. Suddenly he heard a voice: "Come, Rabbi ben Simon, and behold the great grief which has fallen on the house of thy friend, Rabbi Eleazer". Rabbi ben Simon was quite startled, and, walking to the edge of the roof, he saw the messenger and asked him why he was come. The messenger, surprised to see the *old* Rabbi there already, said again: "Come and see the death that has fallen on the house of thy friend, Eleazer". Rabbi ben Simon *began to quake*, but realizing that he who walks by the *sacred* Torah *need never fear*, *he pulled himself together*, took down a stick and set out along the sea-side to the house of his friend, Rabbi Eleazer.'

J (from E):

'About the hour of sunset Rabbi ben Simon sat meditating upon the roof of his house, which was situated by the *shores of the lake*. He continued to meditate, unconscious of the passage of time. Suddenly, a voice cried *from below*: "Rabbi ben Simon, hear the evil which has befallen the house of Rabbi *ben* Eleazer". The old man, startled *from his reverie*, went to the edge of the roof, and looking down, asked the messenger *to repeat his words*. "Death has come to the house of Rabbi *ben* Eleazer", answered the messenger. Then, taking his staff, the old man set out along *the shore of the lake* in the consciousness that whoever follows the *blessed* Torah *can never be overwhelmed by evil*. And he passed on, along the beach to the house of his friend.'

In J, it will be noticed, the place-name has disappeared, and ben Simon is 'startled from his reverie'. In both E and J the examples of direct speech are reduced, and the results of following the Torah are expressed negatively. In another version, at the third remove (K), the house is 'on the walls of Jericho', and the sun is setting 'behind the distant hills'. Rahab (*sic*) ben Simon leans 'over the balcony in silence' when the messenger calls, and 'trembles' when the message is repeated.

II

The parallel series, C, G, N, is as follows:

C (from A):

'One evening, towards sunset, Rabbi ben Simon sat meditating on the roof of his house. Lost in his thoughts, he did not notice the flight of time, and fell asleep. Later, *in* the first watch, a voice spoke to him, and said, "*Arise*, Rabbi ben Simon, and hasten to the house of thy friend, Rabbi Eleazer, for great sadness has descended upon it". Going to the edge of the roof, and looking down, he saw at the foot of the stairs a huddled figure. "I am here", he called. The messenger was surprised to see Rabbi ben Simon up and dressed, and said, "Come quickly. Thy friend, Rabbi Eleazer, has met with swift sickness and sudden death". Rabbi ben Simon hesitated for a moment. "What shall I do?", he pondered, "The time is late, and the journey is far". But his hesitation was only temporary, as he felt it to be *unworthy* of one who walked by the Torah. Taking nothing but his staff, he set out by the sea-side for the house of his friend.'

G (from C):

'One evening *a Rabbi* sat meditating on the roof of his house, when suddenly a voice *within him* spoke *in no uncertain accents*, "Go at once to the house of thy friend. He needs thee. He *is sick*". It was night-time, and how was he to get to the house of his friend? He *began to dress* fully, wrapped his *cloaks* about him, and *hurried down the stairway* from the roof of his house. As he *approached the bottom of the stairs, he stopped short*, for there, huddled up *in a heap*, was a messenger, *who was hardly able to answer his eager inquiries*. "Thy friend is ill; he needs thee". He *did not wait for more*, but set off *as fast as he could* for the home of his sick friend. It was *moonlight*, and he walked along by the sea-shore *as a man with a purpose*.'

N (from G):

'One evening Rabbi ben Simon was sitting on the roof of his house meditating, when suddenly a voice *seemed to say*, "Thy friend is ill; he needs thee". Rabbi ben Simon wondered how he could get to the house of his friend, for it was night. He dressed himself fully, and drew his cloak around him, and hurried down the staircase from above. He had got near the bottom when he stopped short, for lying at the foot was the huddled *body* of the messenger. The messenger was *gasping for breath*, and could hardly speak. "Thy friend is ill and needs thee", he *gasped*. Rabbi ben Simon *strode out*, and it was moonlight. He walked by the side of *the lake* as a man with a *set* purpose.'

In this series the place-name has disappeared at the first remove from A, and the personal names are on the way to extinction.[1] But the most notable change is the way in which the voice becomes an inward voice. This variation is explicit in G, but the way for it is prepared in C. After C, all mention of death ceases, and the plight of the messenger is unexplained. Moonlight is mentioned because in G the scene is pictured and unconsciously dramatized. It is worth noting, however, that, in spite of many changes, the substance of the story remains.

III

Conclusions.

The conclusions set out below are based, not only on the examples given above, but on the full series of fourteen variations.

1. It is obvious that in successive accounts of the story, many points of an explanatory or inferential character are added. Sometimes the additions are quite harmless; at other times they give statements for which there is no warrant.

[1]This would have been still more evident if the name, Rabbi ben Simon, had not been given in each case as a title to the story. As it is, this name disappears in G.

2. Very remarkable is the tendency, in spite of the additions, for the accounts to become shorter. As the table shows, the exceptions to this process are few.

3. Direct speech is replaced by indirect, though not entirely.

4. Personal names and place-names tend to disappear.

5. The form of the later versions becomes rounded and less detailed.

6. In spite of the various changes, the story remains in large measure the same in substance. The additions do not, in most cases, distort the narrative, and sometimes they actually serve to bring the situation more clearly before the mind.

The bearing of such experiments on the study of the Gospel tradition is indicated on p. 124f., where it is claimed that distinctions are possible in the Gospel narratives between those which must have passed through many hands and those which stand nearer to the accounts of eyewitnesses. It has also to be borne in mind that the stories were not only related to individuals, but probably were also told in the first Christian assemblies. While this would make for the possibility of other corruptions, it would also serve to eliminate errors which were merely individual in origin. Moreover, the presence of eyewitnesses, for at least a generation, would serve as a check on corruptions innocently due to the imagination; and, in many cases, hearers would not receive a story from one source alone. The presumption is that the best traditions, in Mark, in Q, and in L, are substantially trustworthy, but that even in these sources every detail cannot be pressed, since room has to be left for reflections and unconscious assumptions on the part of the reporters. In the later traditions, especially in the narratives peculiar to Matthew and the Lukan Birth Stories, apologetic motives, and to some extent, doctrinal interests, become more evident. But even the corrupt traditions of the Apocryphal Gospels may vary from those which are worthless, to those which preserve, not accurate facts, but true religious values.

o

INDEX OF SCRIPTURE PASSAGES

INDEX OF NAMES AND SUBJECTS

215